Circled Money

Thoughts on Economy and Business, Trading and Personal Finance

Copyright © 2016 Nicola Matarese

All rights reserved.

ISBN-13: 978-1546346432

ISBN-10: 1546346430

Circled Money

Thoughts on Economy and Business, Trading and Personal Finance

DEDICATION

To my dad Nando and my mother Iole, who have helped me to become aware of the values of things, those material and not.

Introduction

CONTENTS

INTRODUCTION 5
Hymn to the Capitalism 5
The geometry of fractals: from micro to macro 10
1. SECTION ONE: BASE 18
1.1. FIRST ECONOMIC REVOLUTION: THE SURPLUS 18
1.1.1. Return to Innocence 18
1.1.2. Back To The Future 22
1.2. SECOND ECONOMIC REVOLUTION: THE INDUSTRIAL PRODUCTION 30
1.2.1. The Globalization 30
1.2.2. The Border Between Needs And Desires 33
1.2.3. In the Circle 36
1.2.4. Labor Intensity or Capital Intensity? 39
1.3. THIRD ECONOMIC REVOLUTION: CONNECTIVITY 43
1.3.1. No free meals in economy, nut now cheaper than before 43
1.1.1. Victim Of Our Own Success 47
1.1.2. A Chance for Everyone 48
1.2. FOURTH ECONOMIC REVOLUTION: THE COGNITIVE SYSTEMS ... 52
1.2.1. Transcendence 52
1.2.2. Cognitive Systems: Non-Thinking but Interpreting Machines 55
1.2.3. Flash-Crash 57
2. SECTION TWO: A FINANCIAL INFRASTRUCTURE 63
2.1. THE BANK 63
2.2. THE CIRCLE : WORK REVENUE AND CAPITAL REVENUE 66
2.3. FIRST FUNDAMENTAL LAW OF CAPITALISM 68
2.4. SECOND FUNDAMENTAL LAW OF CAPITALISM 74

Circled Money

Thoughts on Economy and Business, Trading and Personal Finance

2.5.	A FAMILY BUSINESS PLAN	77
3.	SECTION THREE: INVEST WITH PERSONALITY	87
3.1.	GREED & FREEDOM	87
3.1.1.	The beginning of the dream	87
3.1.2.	Finance for Gravity	90
3.1.3.	Trading Volumes	92
3.2.	STRATEGY	97
3.2.1.	Observation	97
3.2.2.	Engaging the Markets	98
3.2.3.	Protection	102
3.3.	EXECUTION	104
3.3.1.	Margin setting	104
3.3.2.	Minimum Business Volumes & Operations	109
4.	CONCLUSION	113
	BIBLIOGRAPHY & DEEPENINGS	117

INTRODUCTION

Hymn to the Capitalism

The picture in the cover is an exercise I did in 2008 when, in an attempt to reinvent my identity and the social and professional life around me, I tried to explore my creative side, tiring of the boring life of a young white collar employee. At that time, my painting subjects were inspired by nights spent with friends in Milan, dinners, and motorbike trips; but the "Freedom's value" on the cover represents continuing thoughts about my life: the driver and the mean of satisfying our passions, happiness, breeding love and pain, crisis and wars.

Gold: the safe haven par excellence, the most recognized mean of universal trading and the historical symbol of desires or riches.

I imagined that we extract it from the blazing bowels of the earth, to melt and it, to shape it, and we treat it to see it as we know it; and the power that we derive from it frees us from the cage of our limits, opening the boundaries of the world; water, air, earth, and again fire and any other combination of these elements. It becomes part of the cyclical nature of our existence

Circled Money

Thoughts on Economy and Business, Trading and Personal Finance

which is portrayed as sea waves and mountain peaks and valleys, like the fluctuations of our financial markets.

That's my vision of the world. It changes through repetition of single and multiple events that we learn to know, we try to predict and of which we enjoy (or suffer) their positive (or negative) effects on our daily life.

Stepping back to the time of my university studies, I believe now that since then, I became more aware of the cyclic nature of our lives; and that happened just by looking at the trends of my moods and how those were affected by external effects.

The dynamics of my personal relationships with friends, colleagues, and acquaintances and the performance of my studies were so unstable that they heavily influenced my personality and my moods with wide swings of excitement to depression, over daily and weekly timeframes.

I was living alone at the time, and without any filter of protection that you have till you are at home, every positive and negative phase was like a financial crash, bouncing and trending spikes and corrections.

In the falling phases, though, I was comforted by my inherent positive thinking with the mindset that in the long term, things tend to get better and the bottom always offers a turning point chance. Sometimes, though, it was hard to hold this on when everything dove deep and went further downward.

With the time, I learned, after a while, to manage the downsides and how to control the following rises as well, containing the "irrational exuberance," relishing the good days, and preparing myself for the next cycle.

In that way of thinking, negative phases put you in a situation to accumulate a buffer of (potential) energy where the greatest opportunities comes from.

From here comes the idea of throwing some thoughts into this book with the aim of sharing my passion for the "happy science" of the economy, developing our capability to make a rational use of money, exploring different perspectives to increase the awareness of our own financial infrastructure and our objectives, getting to the roots of our "Financial Status" and find the reading keys to elaborate the simplest or simplistic solutions, to properly manage our assets.

I am bothered about the spread tendency of many people that seem to take distances from things related to finance, giving to it a general, unjustified, negative facet. People are often reluctant to talk about their salaries, investments or their accounts, or even to

Circled Money

Thoughts on Economy and Business, Trading and Personal Finance

admit that they are passionate about money and tend to connect it to the reasons for our disgraces.

In the quarterly journal of one of the multinational company I worked for, there was once an interview with an executive of the engineering department, where he said that his dream job was to work in the prototyping department. Lies: he received three times the salary of the best-paid guy there, but celebrating the "art of doing" he gave an exemplary company image to other employees and role model to follow. Probably, if he'd said, "I would like to manage our company's pension fund investments" or be the focal point for relationships with the banks, that wouldn't have worked so well. Some could say that loving money is not ethical, and doesn't fit with the ideals and some religious values[1] founded on the fact that money is only one aspect of the reward for having created something;

The aspect for example that is related to the need of having a recognized mean of transaction, to buy something else. In this optic money is always associated to something that we are missing and therefore to an element of dissatisfaction.

---

[1] Matthew 6:24 "No one can serve two masters. Either he will hate the one and love the other, or he will be devoted to the one and despise the other. You cannot serve both God and Money".

Introduction

Imagine how these principles fit with the idea of conceiving the creation of money from the direct result of its availability, which is indeed the foundation of the finance industry. Despite this, I recognize the importance of the economy founded on "labor" but I like also the economy founded on "capital", and will elaborate in this book on how the two elements are connected.

With small commitment and diligent measures, everyone can improve their own wellness, their financial stability and their ability to prepare a prosperous money capital management plan in line with their own goals, needs and personalities.

The best way to start could be to try to make of an instinct, a rational instinct; there will be those who will chase the dream of becoming a home interior designer, others will open child care facilities, or will feed their nautical & sailing passions, while still others will open capital management ventures or will develop luxury hotel properties. We all need to do something that we really like, but backed with a minimum business case weighting the benefits of having the salaried work and the satisfaction to have fed our passions.

Circled Money

Thoughts on Economy and Business, Trading and Personal Finance

The geometry of fractals: from micro to macro

This book itself is an intellectual exercise and an experience that I wanted to give to myself with the hope that it will serve as an inspiration for my future projects, just like drawing the canvas on the book cover, that has been in turn the input for this manuscript.

While writing this book (as was the case with my paintings), I realized that, just after the initial effort, new ideas that come along completely changed the initial purpose. I didn't really know where I would have ended up, but amazingly, the purpose materialized on the way.

Some new ideas have been further developed and adapted to this context, and I kept others, for which I couldn't find a catalyst, in my "Think Tank," ready to go live at the next occasion.

In this effort, I have developed small fragments of ideas and information, originally disconnected, from a number of sources and merged them with the intention of creating something new.

According to Einstein, nothing can be created and nothing can be destroyed: creation is nothing but a combination of primary elements that already exist, raw materials, know-how and time.

Introduction

It's the essence of things more or less complex that are always generated by the union and an organized sequence of these elementary components: those infinitely small and simple.

The atoms that form the molecules, the cells that build the human body, the thousands of components that make up an airplane, the lines of code that generate a software, the sequences of notes - those infinitive combinations that make a melody and a song; the sequence of appropriate letters that form a word and an array of words that form an idea, a message, a theory and so on.

When we go in a furniture store, our attention is attracted by the displayed and complete assembled product; we imagine it at home in the place we have in mind with our knick-knacks and so on. Then we decide to buy it, and we get the sub-assemblies' kit that we bring home.

We unpack them, observe the confusion of pieces on the floor, and feel downhearted (at least, the first few times), thinking of the difference between the finished product that we saw in the exposition and that whole confusing array of components on the floor. Then you start with the instructions and prepare the first table, insert the pins, screws and nuts, perform the same operation on four boards, and behold: the first cube starts to

Circled Money

Thoughts on Economy and Business, Trading and Personal Finance

represent the drawer, a shelf, a library, or a cabinet. At the end, almost magically, following the sequence of the booklet, here we go: we have something similar to what we chose to buy.

My idea is that we need to learn to understand also the importance of single and small components, that at a first glance might be overlooked, and manage them with the purpose of creating added value.

The sensitivity of understanding the opportunities hidden in the "micro-world" will give us the change to develop simple elements and put them together in a way that we can materialize an idea.

Just like individual concepts which make this book, small steps and micro hints will help and stimulate our imagination to reach our target - or, at least, make a try for it.

Have you ever thought about how "the theory of games" could provide guidelines for strategic decisions, or the importance of the prime numbers on which Ramanujan worked for all his life, or the number of physical and quant theories or formulas that, at a first glance, seem far away from their practical applications?

With this book, I will try to short-circuit some improbable connections, in some cases forcing hands as well; with the risk to affect its reading fluency. For the readers that will find

Introduction

inconsistencies and unjustified complexity of the arguments treated here, I can just ask to give always a second chance and try another time to see things from different perspectives. If you want you will find an inspiration from the concepts that you will find wrong, and that is positive anyway.
As I did here, I like to take dares; when it goes well, I feel good.
I once took inspiration from a guy I met to sell him my motorbike for 1,500 Euros. He was a tall guy, slim figure, around 30 years old, blue eyes and curly hairs of Ukrainian mother and Italian father, well dressed (except shoes); I noticed his dirty nails and he was driving an old Volkswagen caravan-hippy style with a Polish car plate. While talking, he told me that he would have resold my motorbike in Poland with a gain of 100 euros. Exactly: one hundred euros only, after clearing custom duties, transportation fees, and registration in Poland. Then he started telling me about the number of motorbikes he used to trade: two loads of 20 motorbikes a month. Then he told me that he was a representative for an encyclopedia publishing house, he also marketed food products made in Italy with the Russians and other occasional opportunities. While I was torn between wanting to end the deal or walking away because I was beginning question his story, I was amazed by how creative people can be.

Circled Money
Thoughts on Economy and Business, Trading and Personal Finance

In the end, I sold it, and thought at how to get something good from that experience.

The 1'500 Euro I gained with that deal were almost nothing compared to the that mind openness I wanted to start to follow.

I wanted to try to augment my capacity of being receptive to multiple sources and interests to find new routes, open new doors, creating new connections, new ideas.

This book will impart some of my experiences and relationships with money.

I will tell about my personal view on economy and finance, the value of labor and its price, the differences between a cost and an investment.

I will give hints on how to manage risks, hold on a difficult situation or run away, and, in the worst case, how to handle losses, real and virtual (and accumulate potential energy [2]).

In the first section, you will find a quick description of what I believe have been the most important historical economic revolutions, from agriculture to the spread of semantic software. In some cases, I'll go into the details of a business plan providing representative case figures but just to help to

---
[2] Just think about a loaded spring

understand the order of magnitudes for the topics we are talking about.

In the second section, I suggest a way to frame and build our own financial infrastructure to become better aware of the importance of an economic-financial stability and develop a family business-management plan. I tried to provide some tools for a better control of assets and a sustainable distribution of expenditures to get the most effective balance between fixed incomes & outcomes (salaries & costs) and variable incomes & outcomes (capital revenues and investments)[3].

In the last part, I tried to break down the value of time and work in an attempt to provide methods for properly managing monetary resources to invest in the financial markets through three steps: observation, engagement, and protection.

This method is based on a mixture of a discretionary approach supported by observation of market behavior and some principles from automatic trading (HFT - High Frequency Trading). This will help to identify recurring trends and the continuous setup of technical "supports" and "resistances" to

---

[3] In the tables and simulations please forgive any simplification on the boundary conditions, but just consider the high level principles.

Circled Money
Thoughts on Economy and Business, Trading and Personal Finance

run semi-automatic buy and sell transactions between these value bands.

Before we operate in the financial market though, we need first to pass through a thought selection of financial products that in the long term hold the highest likelihood of generating value (Joel Grenblatt's method[4]) together with a method inspired to the Martingale, applied in specific timeframes.

At the same time, we can follow a "straddle trading" approach buying two financial products that move in opposite directions (by either opening simultaneous long – short on the same product, or buying products that usually go in opposite directions, like gasoline vs. natural gas).

This might seem to be a Zero Value strategy (the gains from one are eaten from the loss on the other), but we will see that even in this worst case situation, this approach can have its positive side. In Economy, nothing is granted (there are "no free meals"), but engaging the financial market with favorable probabilities is certainly the only method to achieve success.

---

[4] The Little Book That Still Beats the Market – September 7, 2010 by Joel Greenblatt

Introduction

You will find many formulas and numbers, those specifically related to personal assumptions and direct or indirect experience, with the purpose of just giving a better impression to the reader, on how close to the standards these cases are, and how can they fit with everyone's situation (if for example your revenue is double than the one used in the case study, you can just apply factor two and run the simulation again).

Circled Money

Thoughts on Economy and Business, Trading and Personal Finance

1. SECTION ONE: BASE

1.1. FIRST ECONOMIC REVOLUTION: THE SURPLUS

1.1.1. Return to Innocence

The first economic revolution came more than 10,000 years ago, when the prey man-hunted and the resources that he had directly from the earth became insufficient to satisfy his primary needs of feeding himself. With the agriculture, he invented a system to produce quantity of goods in excess of those merely needed for his subsistence. In this way he also discovered the first form of Capital Stock; the surplus, whose concept drove the human society of those times to radical changes, and first appearance of the principles of a true economy. The availability of exceeding goods imposed a management system more projected to the future the moved people to develop new principles of relationships, based on longer term visions, and tools to manage them over time.

New stakeholders came-up along - the producer, the buyer, the seller, the accountant - who developed new facilities (warehouses, barns) and transaction systems and rules.

They invented debt and credit and a new monetary system was established, which was guaranteed by the sovereign institution and regulatory entities that were also created to the purpose.

Many technological solutions were also developed like plows, for example, or irrigation systems and crop preservation techniques, along with chemistry, medicine, and so on.

All the system moved around the primary goods from the earth that satisfied our basic needs, to feed ourselves and our families, to preserve health, and, at the same time, to provide an important catalyst to social life and cultural identity.

Food is since ever the most important value and was the first mean of transaction for the primary necessity of keeping us alive, the main natural instinct of humankind.

Medicine did a lot, of course; but how much stronger or healthier have we become with the huge varieties of products we eat nowadays?

Just think about the average lifespan in the western world, which almost tripled over the latest 2,000 years, and the social value associated with meals for family, friends and business.

Sadly we have to recognize though that there are populations in certain geographic areas of the world for which food availability is still not enough to satisfy the basic needs.

Circled Money

Thoughts on Economy and Business, Trading and Personal Finance

On the other side most of us are invaded by a such huge offer of goods that we are often unaware of their quality, origins, production processes and supply chain. The battle to reduce selling prices and/or increase margins unfortunately led to situations, where food became recently also causes of malaise and sickness. The problem is capturing the attention of many organization (like the EFSA), but the diffusion of knowledge is still not sufficient to raise the level of consciousness of the vast majority of the world's population.

The culture of "quality food" is not spread out enough to allow for investment to further develop it, and therefore "mass food" still remains cheap enough to maintain its predominant role, notwithstanding it holds health safety hazards.

As we will see later on in this book, while I have solid arguments to justify and support a sustainable industrial globalization, when we talk about the agriculture, I have just one sufficient simple element against it. Globalization itself means big distances, and even with express transportation, the primary elements of "quality food" (freshness, traceability of the supply chain and geographical awareness) are the first to lose their essence.

In fact, natural goods are strictly interconnected with the territorial geography and organic characteristics of the earth and its environment, the culture of managing the land, and the rules and regulation of local government as well as health and safety policies. The technological evolution of mass production, even if it brings undisputed benefits on one hand, also drives the abuse of natural resources and brings situations of ethical and environmental distress (the Bovine Spongiform Encephalopathy (BSE) in Europe few years ago, just to name one for instance).

Notwithstanding this, the technology played a fundamental role for the development of food industry, mainly on transformation process of natural elements which at the end make the core value of the final product. As we will also see in Section Two, while industrial globalization is characterized by a relative inter-independence between capital assets and labor [5] (where marginal productivity is proportional to the availability of labor and capital), in agriculture it is the exact opposite, and the increase of either capital and/or labor might not always entail higher production.

---

[5] Infinite elasticity of the production function means complete flexibility of the ratio capital and labor. Null elasticity means that the production is a given by the fixed amount of capital and labor, and the increase of one of the two will not provide any additional benefit (nil marginal productivity).

Circled Money

Thoughts on Economy and Business, Trading and Personal Finance

1.1.2. Back To The Future

A wider universal reward of the importance of the enhancement of nutritive properties and a spread of agriculture sustainable mechanization can increase the culture of Quality Eating and promote a shorter supply chain (at the best, from the producer to the consumer).

This may launch the base for a new food economy grounded on ethical principles, fostering a healthy environment and holding direct and indirect benefits at all levels (such as national healthcare systems, insurances, and productivity at work as well as overall wellness and quality of life).

Niche productions have attracted a lot of interest, as they require scientific contributions at specialist level both in regard to genetic conservation and the cultivation technique.

These are activities that bring us into a well-defined territorial context, with the logic of production oriented to the enhancement of product quality. This could be the beginning of research into the agriculture of the future and holds a huge potential for a sustainable and prosperous business.

The guarantee of a "quality production" characterized by the absence of substances and residues that are harmful to health, though, may not be sufficient to make the product attractive enough without the help of a strong marketing/awareness campaign. This may guarantee bigger volumes to trigger economy of scale and raise its price competitiveness upon the following principles.

1. Ecological/environmental: to comply with principles that govern the relationship between living organisms and what is around them and aim to preserve and improve environmental quality (for example maintaining or increasing soil fertility, biodiversity and biological activity, avoiding the use of toxics and minimizing pollution and creating a harmonious balance between crop production and livestock).
2. Ethological: in respect of the physiological and ethological needs of the animal, ensuring living conditions that allow animals to express the basic, innate aspects of their behavior.
3. Ethics: to develop a respect sense for nature and the intrinsic value of domestic animals as well as human rights to produce high-quality food. This implies the need to develop an aesthetically attractive farming landscape to provide all those who are involved in organic farming and processing with a quality of life that meets their needs.

Circled Money
Thoughts on Economy and Business, Trading and Personal Finance

4. Ergonomic. to ensure the establishment of a work environment that is safe, secure, and healthy for farmers and the employed staff.
5. Economical. to foster use of the most renewable resources possible, which generate an income sufficient for the farmer while offering a fair price to the consumer.

As almost every summer, I spend part of my holiday in Sicily and make occasional visits to friends and relatives living in the inner landscapes.

There is one of the farm I visited where the Limousine Cows were raised. They are particularly indicated both for their ability to adapt to the territory and for the excellent organoleptic characteristics of their meat. The farmer gave me a very clear and detailed explanation of his job, while tasting a good spread of choices of amazing cheese and meat, red wine after a short walking outside at 36 Celsius degrees. I had to do some research afterwards to tidy up my ideas but it was a good insight for me to get fashioned about it and keep my interest for the topic alive. The cows conceive and give birth according to nature there, in large pastures, meadows and woods. Each herd is composed of cows one or two bulls and calves, which are nursed by the mother until the age of 7 or 8 months.

Already from the first month of age, the calves learn to graze on fresh grass and to socialize among their peers, forming characteristic "play groups". Their diet is balanced according to their age: cattle intended for slaughter, approximately 60 a year, are fed with fodder, barley, corn, broad beans, and organic peas.

Bulls and mares feed exclusively on grass. In the winter period of December-April, they are fed only with the forage produced in the farm: 7.5 kg of hay and 15 kg of green haylage. Even grazing in winter, the herd has about 16 kg per day of hay in bale feeders. The breeding heifers are manually fed with 6 kg hay and 3 kg of a mixture of cereals and they receive 25% more than the standard ratio above.

The calves (from 3 months to 8 months) are let out along with the mothers and are fed with hay a and 2.5 kg of a mixture of cereals and beans. They are then separated and fed with 6 kg of hay and a mixture consisting of barley, corn, and beans.

He also described some processes and the work to be carried out to maintain the infrastructures like cleaning the stables, their renovation and maintenance. He had to take care of the organization of the work, material and water. There is the necessity of making a wise stock management (feed, hay and re-ordering processes) and conduct inspections to ensure daily

Circled Money

Thoughts on Economy and Business, Trading and Personal Finance

breeding of the cattle, test pregnancy and deliveries and make a continued assessment of the state of health of the calf and the mare.

It is required to also straw handling and manage for an optimal use of organic manure and fertilizers as well as tractors and machines, including their remittance at the end of use.

He must organize storage for equipment, spare parts, fuel, oils to ensure their ready availability. As far as the Pastures are concerned the activities include fences installation, periodic checks and their replacement when damaged. He makes a careful installation of electric wires around fences and ensure their connections, continuity, and the voltage and ensure sufficient availability of water. It is absolutely important to manage calves births like: recording stages of pregnancy, registering births, sex, and again perform health checks for young calves .

There is a lot of work to manage crops and make the land preparation, breakage, harrowing, rolling, sowing, organic fertilization, manure as well as packaging, displacing the bales in the field transport to barn fodder accommodations.

With these high level inputs and some further assumptions, I tried to build his business cases to figure out the right price for a Kg of produced meet. I dove myself in quite a difficult exercise that I believed to have brilliantly resolved and decided to share it with him after two weeks. I have to admit that I am still not sure if his reaction was more close to surprise or disconcert in front to the confusing numbers I showed him. I tried in fact to rationalize a system functioning since decades (perhaps centuries) by traditions, hard work experience, social dynamics, weather and seasonal events, building up a small financial model.

At the end we didn't go into the details but we had good time together again. For those readers interested to the detailed analysis, I defined the following boundary conditions:

Business Environment and Boundary Conditions	Qty
Land extension (hectars)	70
Production and cost analysis timeframe (year)	1
Nr. mares (unit)	67
Average life of 1 mare	10
Number of Produced Calves Per Year (unit)	57
Weight at slaughter (kg)	500
Weight at value 60% (kg)	300
Bales production over 70 hectars	800
Kg of haybale per day for one mare over one year (kg)	16
Kg of haybale per day for one calf over one year (kg)	6
Number of bales per year needed by one mare (unit)	6
Number of bales per year needed by one calf (unit)	6
Bale production cost	€ 71.64
Manhour	€ 15.00
Cost gasoline per liter	€ 0.80
Bale weight (kg)	365

And compiled three data sheets with the breakdown of the major costs affecting the production and preparation of 1 Kg of meat.

Circled Money

Thoughts on Economy and Business, Trading and Personal Finance

FEEDING COSTS							
SEEDS COST	cost per kg	kg per hectar		cost per hectar		cost for 70 hectars per year	
Alfalfa/Luscerne (every 5 years)	52	40		€ 208.00	€ 41.60	€ 2912	€ 2912
FORAGE PRODUCTION	manhour per hectar in hr	gasoline consumption per hectar in Lt	cost manhour per hectar		cost gasoline per hectar	cost for 70 hectars per year	€ 57316
Hay chopping	0.8	1.95	€ 12.00		€ 1.56	€ 949	
Natural fertilization	1.6	1.78	€ 24.00		€ 1.42	€ 1780	
Milling	1.8	4.89	€ 27.00		€ 3.91	€ 2164	
Ground Preparation	1.4	2.5	€ 21.00		€ 2.00	€ 1610	
Sowing	0.6	1.51	€ 9.00		€ 1.21	€ 715	
Crops and packaging	35	151.08	€ 525.00		€ 120.86	€ 45210	
Displacement and stock	4.3	6.66	€ 64.50		€ 5.33	€ 4888	
Total	**45.5**	**170.37**	**€ 682.50**		**€ 136.30**	**€ 57316**	
PASTURE MAINTENANCE	manhour per hectar in hr	gasoline consumption per hectar in Lt	cost manhour per hectar		cost gasoline per hectar	cost for 70 hectars per year	€ 24563
Natural soil fertilization (10 times a year)	8	8.89	€ 120.00		€ 7.11	€ 8898	
Hay chopping (10 times a year)	6	26.66	€ 90.00		€ 21.33	€ 7793	
Forest status checks and maintenance (10 times a year)	1.5	0.44	€ 22.50		€ 0.35	€ 1600	
Wood collection and transportation (10 times a year)	1.5	6.66	€ 22.50		€ 5.33	€ 1948	
Fence Maintenance (once a year)	4	2.22	€ 60.00		€ 1.78	€ 4324	
Total	**21**	**44.87**	**€ 315.00**		**€ 35.90**	**€ 24563**	
OTHER COSTS FOR FOOD							€ 55559
Supplementary feed	€ 37000						
Land rental costs	€ 8000						
Machinery depreciation	€ 10759						
Total	€ 55559						
TOTAL COST FOR FEEDING	€ 140'349						
TOTAL COST FOR FEEDING PER CALF	€ 2462						
COST PER KG MEAT SOLD	€ 8.21						

OTHER COSTS							
OTHER COSTS							€ 25569
G&A	€ 25569						
TOTAL OTHER COST	€ 25'569						
TOTAL OTHER COST PER CALF	€ 449						
COST PER KG MEAT SOLD	€ 1.50						

SLAUGHTERING COSTS

TREATMENT	cost		cost for 57 calves	
Slaughtering and scrap dismissal	€	150.00	€	8550.00
Manhour slaughter	€	100.00	€	5700.00
Manhour for packaging	€	80.00	€	4560.00
Manhour for deliveries	€	40.00	€	2280.00
Fuel for deliveries	€	50.00	€	2850.00
Packaging	€	60.00	€	3420.00
Total	€	**480.00**	€	**27360.00**
				€ 27360

FIXED COSTS				
Laboratory rental fees	€	1200.00		
Laboratory costs	€	4500.00		
Truck expenses	€	8000.00		
Other depreciations	€	5959.00		
Total	€	**19659**		
				€ 19659

TOTAL COST FOR SLAUGHTERING	€ 47019
TOTAL COST FOR SLAUGHTERING PER CALF	825
COST PER KG MEAT SOLD	€ 2.75

BREEDING COSTS

CALVES PRODUCTION	cost	Yearly quote for 67 mares	
purchase cost of 1 mare	€ 1800.00		
purchase cost of 1 mare over one year	€ 180.00	€ 120600.00	
			€ 120960

MANHOUR	nr people	hr/day	days	hrs/year	Total manhour cost per year
Winter period	2	6	180	2160	€ 32400
Summer period	1	6	180	1080	€ 16200
Transumahnce (every 10days during the 6 months in summer)	2	2	18	72	€ 1080
Total				**3312**	€ **49680**
					€ 49680

OTHER COSTS FOR BREEDING		
machinery deprecations	€	10858
		€ 10858

TOTAL COST OF BREEDING	€ 72598
TOTAL COST FOR BREEDING PER CALF	€ 1274
COST PER KG MEAT SOLD	€ 4.25

| TOTAL COST PER KG MEAT | € 16.70 |

Circled Money

Thoughts on Economy and Business, Trading and Personal Finance

1.2. SECOND ECONOMIC REVOLUTION: THE INDUSTRIAL PRODUCTION

1.2.1. The Globalization

The industrial revolution launched the basis for approaching a manufacturing activity by processes with the target of minimizing costs, expanding the accessibility to goods that, if made by artisans, were only for a few wealthier consumers. Together with progressive globalization, it was the greatest step towards consumer democratization.

In fact, the technological progress, together with a greater manpower availability and labor organization systems, prompted the evolution from "work in series" principle to a "work in parallel" production system.

The work has been progressively broken down in multiple simple tasks allowing the single operator to specialize himself in single unitary work-steps.

In this way the final product and its inherent properties came from the development, assembly and integration of "smaller", "elementary" components, of a multitude of single simple tasks, which, for this reason, are easier to improve.

According to the economic theory of Adam Smith in the Wealth of Nations, the division of labor plays a role of paramount importance in the development and production capacity of a given manufacturing system, because the division of work increases the ability of a worker to perform a particular work-step and reduces dead time due to passing the worker from one operation to the next.

Let's take an example of a generic good (one screw and one bolt, tightened together) manufactured with a process composed of two stages (in two stations) without division of labor and a production rate, for example, of 20 pieces per hour.

In the first stage (A) the bolts are put in their position on the jig, and in the second stage (B) the screws are added and tightened. The two operations take place in two different stations of the workshop.

One operator picks the bolts up and put them in their pre-set places in the jig. Thereafter, the same operator and the jig move to the next station (dead-time, or t1) to match the screws and tighten them. At the end of this second operation he returns to the previous station (dead time, or t2) to start working on the next product.

For each product, the recorded time delay equals to t1+t2. If the workshop had two workers who behaved in the same way, the time delay would be multiplied by two and if the workers used common

Circled Money

Thoughts on Economy and Business, Trading and Personal Finance

resources (such as the same workbenches), it would also add the problem of queues.

According to the English economist, labor's productivity may increase by a different organization of tasks. By entrusting the first worker only to his task on the bolt and the second one on the screws, neither of the two move from their places of work (stations). Only the units of semi-finished product are then supposed to move and the two workers don't interfere by moving or sharing the same space.

In the course of time, the first worker specializes in operations on the bolt, because it performs only that task. This specialization of labor means that the first worker can complete more units of product in a given timeframe because he is more skillful, faster, and makes fewer errors. The same happens to the second operator with the screws. Both workers have become more productive and the division of labor has increased the productivity of each worker from 20 to 30 pieces produced per hour of work, against the same invested capital and means of production (always the same two workbenches and two people).

Let's look at what happened in China around the first years after the year 2000.

Beside other typical aspects inherent to that society and social systems, their huge amount of available manpower allowed to break down work into simple micro tasks for which worker's skills requirements were reduced to a minimum and therefore at minimal cost. Overall costs went down, production outputs increased, and the western world, even when losing jobs, got access to cheaper Plasma or LCD TVs, faster computer processors, textiles, furniture. Those, like anything else materialized from the creativity of advanced countries, could be given for production to these high labor intensity countries and get spread to world's consumers at more affordable prices than before.

1.2.2. The Border Between Needs And Desires

I read once a story on a newspaper on a talk between two friends: "A few days ago, my son got married. He is an employee like I was at his age and also his wife works. They tell me that today that one salary is not enough. Now, the question is: when I married in 1969, my salary was not high, my wife was not working but I could maintain a family. Now the statistics tell me that we are much wealthier than before. Why then, was my salary enough for me and my wife back then, while today it is not adequate?"

Circled Money

Thoughts on Economy and Business, Trading and Personal Finance

I think that complaining about money with parents is almost a natural behavior but the issue there depends more on living standards that we pretend.

When we were kids we played tennis with heavy wooden rackets of 700 gr. Today we use ultralight aerospace grade carbon fiber rackets and anti-vibration features to prevent tennis elbow..

If today I get out and I realize I've forgotten my mobile phone, I would feel like I hadn't worn my winter jacket on the 29th of January or left home my glasses to drive on the highway at night.

Almost everyone nowadays has a car and all cars have park aids, distance sensors, ABS, and other features which back then were considered a luxury.

When I was 7 years old, my mother used to trim and tailor our older friends clothes, jackets and carnival costumes as well.

In short, if the son in the story above lived with the same 1969 goods and services then, his salary would be more than enough.

But those goods and services do not exist anymore, even if he wanted them, and the living standards now require[6] "everything and more" at the same cost.

---

[6] The Classical economists said that "supply creates its own demand".

I am writing these lines on that same day that Trump became the US president, and I am more and more convinced that his anti-globalization principles are economically wrong.

Why should I care to defend the relocation of manufacturing factories or want to save the job market if the goods produced are so expensive that I cannot afford them?

This is probably what the western world's people thought before deciding to do outsourcing in low-cost countries, and this is what the Chinese workers, the Indians, or the Pakistani people perhaps think when they go to their workplace. Some youths of western world may strive to find a job, but they have high level education from high school and university, eats three times a day, go out on Saturday evenings, and have 4G smartphones. The average low-cost county's youth work 14 hours a day, 2$ a day salary and have very low possibility to own the products that they themselves contribute to produce.

You will agree that every man is rich or poor to the extent that he is able to procure his means of subsistence, stay comfortable, and enjoy the pleasures of life. The question is: for how long will this still be true for us Italians, Americans, British, Germans and so on? Outsourcing is fine as long as this gives the western world the opportunity, time, and the necessary resources to focus on higher

Circled Money

Thoughts on Economy and Business, Trading and Personal Finance

added value activities (Research & Development); otherwise, the fun will be soon over.

The production facilities located in developing countries will likely begin to have their own centers of creativity, and the probability that the next technological breakthrough will occur in what is currently defined the industrialized world, is falling steeply.

Considering the increase in the level of education and professional training in developing countries as well as our know-how and technology transfers to them, today's emerging countries will also themselves begin to make innovations.

This will probably mean a cost increase and a new push to find other sources of low-cost mass production that could remain commercially attractive (just look at what China is doing in Ethiopia and other south-Saharan regions), at least till new opportunities will rise from another big worldwide crisis.

1.2.3. In the Circle

Every employer, at least in principle, would like to have their workers perform like robots without psychological problems, holidays, or opinions - only performance.

If ever this would be possible the whole economic system would run at the maximum efficiency with production at minimal costs.

In a purely competitive environment, the low cost of the product lowers the margins and the only way to compensate it would be an increase of the production rates.

On the long term such system, together with the abundance of the offer range, would hardly be of any value without innovation. Would you really care of having the 4th Cathodic Ray Tube TV in your 3 bedroom flat?

As further explored in the next section of this book, when there is no gain, there is no marginal utility and no interest in producing

Without margins, the companies will be unable to pay their debts. They'll close and dismiss their employees and they will not have money to buy other products from other companies. Other companies will see their profits going down, and will close too. Other employees will be laid off, and all will lead towards a deflationary spiral. The world is over and your 4th TV is the last of your problems.

Recovery comes when the strongest survivors begin to re-invest in production activities and following sales, at reduced costs from the effect of the crisis itself, generating profits and putting the system in motion again. In a climate of renewed optimism, the reduction of labor costs contributes to the same recovery, as well as access to credit. The banks "create" and lend money to allow the producer

Circled Money

Thoughts on Economy and Business, Trading and Personal Finance

of a particular good to buy equipment and power their business (again increasing quantities and reducing costs). And here, again, we have new technologies, new processes, new machines, more production, and another crisis.

Creativity, design and development, prototyping and first series launches are the grounds for our continued growth. Creativity is an ingredient in the production that still makes a difference to the industrialized world. It is clear that a country, region, laboratory, or a university that demonstrates the capability for great inventions, innovations, and improvements of the standards will appear in situations where workers and researchers are in close contact with knowledge and, of course, a sparkling capital investment activity.

However, the increasing costs of feeding the creative side of new technologies often linked to advanced infrastructures, working equipment, are also connected to higher hiring costs.

The increasing demands of engineers and scientists, entails the need to select and outsource part of the work, the less noble portion, to other places where wages and prices have not yet been raised by economic success.

To come back to the question on the 4th Cathodic Ray Tube TV, the answer is: for sure we will not want it but if you could have one 3D LED or Curve TV's, perhaps we can think about it.

1.2.4. Labor Intensity or Capital Intensity?

In my professional experience in the aerospace environment, at the beginning of any new design and development project of an aircraft or one of its subsystem, we always needed to decide on the levels of involvement of suppliers.

We may have several cases but the two extremes are:

1. a procurement approach by systems (one supplier only for a complete system – the hydraulic system for example where the same supplier delivers the pump with the ducts and the valves all integrated, also said Tier 1) or
2. a procurement approach at components level (ie.: one supplier for the pump, one for the ducts, one for the valve).

In the first case, the supplier takes a big part of the aircraft and has the responsibility and liability of managing their own suppliers in cascade effect. The Aircraft OEM (Original Equipment Manufacturer) will have a higher procurement prices for its systems, but lower exposure in terms of internal cost. Managing the different systems integration and the interfaces between ten big suppliers is not as critical as it would be if we approached the project at its component level (second case) with hundreds of suppliers.

Circled Money

Thoughts on Economy and Business, Trading and Personal Finance

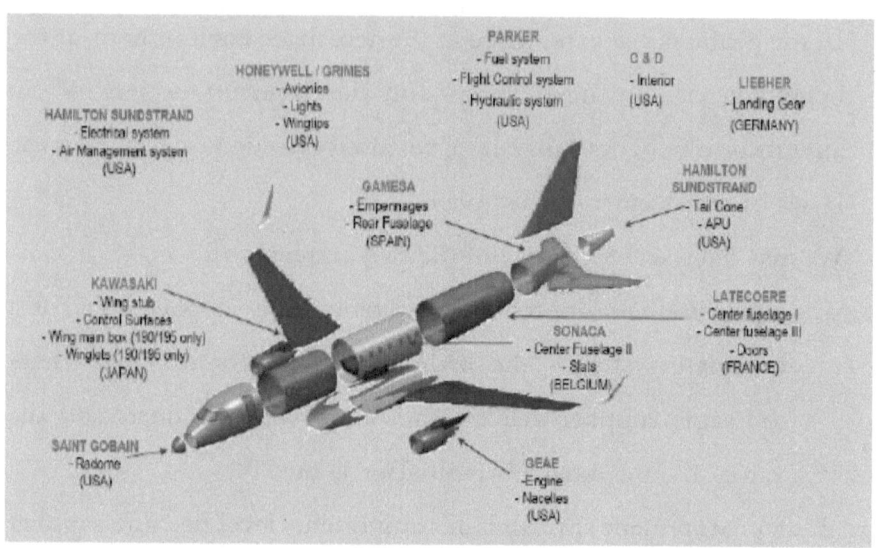

Figure 1. Risk Sharing Partnerships of the ERJ – 170/190 Program
Source: Embraer Company

In the latter scenario, by going directly to the source, the procurement price will be definitely lower, but the integration of single actuators, electronic boxes, and tip-to-tail pipes and electrical wires will doubtless be higher.

When we talk about the integration of two systems or two components, this means thousands of hours of design, adjustments, documentations, laboratory and aircraft tests on ground and in the air, and multiple trial and error loops.

For an aircraft of 5 million dollars, the investment can be 50 times higher.

Project Cost	Percentage
Internal Man-Hours (R&D and Management)	50%
Suppliers and Outsourcing Engineering, Tests, Prototypes	40%
Manufacturing Jigs and Tools	8%
Marketing	2%

Aircraft Costs	Percentage
Bill Of Materials	70%
Transport	1%
Internal Manufactured Parts	20%
Internal Man-hours Structural Assy (Man hours)	2%
Internal Man-hours Wire Harnesses (Man hours)	1%
Internal Man-hours System Integration, Completion, Paint (Man hours)	5%
Flight Testing	1%

How these 250 million (the 5 million times 50) are split between internal and external costs will also be part of the company's strategy, depending on currency exchange rates between different countries, overall business health, and expectations. With the level of technology today, it is impossible to have an OEM aircraft manufacturer who is able to build his own structural parts, (in aluminum or composite), engines, avionics, and tires; just to name a few. Such completely vertical, integrated aerospace company capable of designing, developing, producing an aircraft and

Circled Money

Thoughts on Economy and Business, Trading and Personal Finance

supporting it in the aftermarket, would have a huge size, with inherent large management costs, complex processes, bigger infrastructures and wide financial exposure. On the other hand, they will have the complete design know-how and knowledge of production, and will be completely independent.

How that worth, for the assembly of metal parts rather than the integration of an entire avionic bay, is part of the decision to go with Labor intensive or Capital intensive work, but I believe the concept is clear.

We are, therefore, in the middle of the battlefield between "outsourcing", to contain costs and focus on high added value activities, and the "vertical integration" to preserve the full know-how.

1.3. THIRD ECONOMIC REVOLUTION: CONNECTIVITY

1.3.1. No free meals in economy, nut now cheaper than before

An old Chinese saying suggests: "If you want to create wealth, create roads". At the beginning the ancient Egyptians and then the Romans expanded their dominion with the enormous benefit that they derived from their ability to sail in the Mediterranean and develop their roads.

In 1500 Venice was the most prosperous city in Europe thanks to the business market as a meeting point for Eastern and Western cultures, and in the 17th century Great Britain was the greatest empire of history thanks to the power of its fleets. The invention of the combustion engine, the first cars, railroads, electricity and then radio, telephone, cinema, television, air transport, electronics and computer science are other aspects of how communications technology evolved and spread all over the world

The development of the communication systems till the point as we know them today offered a continued raising opportunity to trade and expand the markets.

Circled Money

Thoughts on Economy and Business, Trading and Personal Finance

Purchasing and sales markets have found in this way the right resources or the right customer, and allowed to close business deals quicker and with minimal costs.

Without even considering the cultural and social benefits gained by crossing the borders of knowledge, the easier exchange of information has allowed us to optimize any trade activity, reducing inflation and stimulating competition.

When we buy something we exchange an asset for cash. We are ready to give away that money because we think that the utility that we derive from that purchase is greater than the sacrifice (or "uselessness") of giving away our money.

When we have closed a transaction, how could we be sure to have obtained the best deal value from a transaction and that we couldn't fetch a better price for it? In a perfect competitive environment, classical economics has an answer: the price we found with the full visibility of the market is the best that could get.

Besides the fact that it is in the interest of the butcher or the greengrocer behind the corner to give us the best products at the best prices in order not to lose our fidelity, the question is whether there is perfect competition or not.

In fact, if we look at the market situation from a broader perspective, our grocery store is the closest to where I live. Perhaps I know the owner and I like talking to him from time to time, and that place would likely be my preference even if I had to pay a small extra fee.

The fact that you are aware or not of this surcharge is, however, another complex element of this topic.

To better understand it, we will have to do market research, make phone calls, and maybe drive some miles so that we'll probably burn, in advance, the extra costs that we originally anticipated to save; plus time and stress. Today, with computer science and telecommunications, the cost of information (if we do not consider the time spent on our research) is almost null.

At the base of an effective market research, information plays an essential role; be it to buy clothes or a flight ticket or the shares of a company (in the latter case however there are now some exceptions due to the HFT as we will see in the next chapter).

What internet has done is to make the competition, even if not perfect, less imperfect than before, giving the buyer more opportunity to look for the best product at the best price.

The same is true for a bag shop: at one time this never sold the bags as he could, due to a not favorable location of the store or

Circled Money

Thoughts on Economy and Business, Trading and Personal Finance

the limited space for the exhibition of its products, while now it is possible to have potential customers from all over the world and serve them at the same time.

In the same way the buyers, can use search engines and know how many and which bags are available all over the world.

Not surprisingly, online purchases have been increasing exponentially, and this phenomenon has pushed the vast majority of companies to acquire their own e-commerce solutions.

A digital business model, in addition to any other channel of traditional sales, has become a necessity, holding remarkable objective advantages:

• It saves time

• It allows, in a simple and fast way, to compare prices

• It opens the market worldwide, presenting a wider range of choice and opportunity.

Amazon, eBay, Airbnb, Cocontest, Zooppa, Home Restaurant, Etsy, Toluna, Udemy O Skillshare, Smartpassiveincome, Trnd, and Paypershopping, just to name a few, are some interesting sharing economy cases I found, which represent incomparable ingenuity.

Any one of them represents a perfect competition example and, of course, a business potentiality.

1.1.1. Victim Of Our Own Success

In a conference held in 1928, Keynes described the phenomenon of technological progress as our greatest opportunity to break away from work commitments and devote ourselves to philosophy and other recreational activities, enjoying a week of 20 working hours while maintaining the same productivity. That didn't really happen, but with the simplification of many tasks, surrounding our daily lives (like a post office line, or any other activity that we call "noise elements"), we could focus on higher, more valuable interests, be happier and have deeper stimulus for creativity and productivity.

In my office, I spend between 30 and 50 percent of my time just reading and processing emails, and I look at my email accounts up to 15 hours a day - sometimes even on holidays. It is expected that since so many tasks have become much simpler, replying to an email on Sundays doesn't take anything out from our free time.

Often, but not always, replying to emails during the week end is our choice; which is a win, anyway.

Simply we are aware that with the same level of commitment and effort, we have the possibility to generate more value than before; and that's great. The work in the future is not going to be about full-time employment. In the next decades, millennials will hold

Circled Money

Thoughts on Economy and Business, Trading and Personal Finance

senior positions. They will bring with them the mentality that work doesn't need to be 9am-to-5pm; nor does it have to be conducted in an office space. People want freedom and flexibility. They want to be in charge of their own destiny.

However we take it, new technologies and their progress, thanks to, or because of their success, have erased all borders between work and leisure, work and rest, and work and travel.

1.1.2. A Chance for Everyone

For those like me that in the latest years experienced the worst financial disaster ever seen, the third revolution offered no better time to reinvent ourselves, get out from our "comfort zone" and take advantages from it. The collapse of the cost of information has made the whole process more efficient, allowing us put ourselves in situations where almost everyone wins. For example, it is very simple to create an online shop, and it does not require high technological skills. The most important thing is to have nice photos of the products we want to sell, and have the patience to create the right descriptions. Selling on Ebay is very simple: you can start with a relatively low investment (from 19,95 € up to 39,00 € per month). Recently Amazon, one of the largest sellers of electronic commerce in the world, has proved to be the first in enterprise web & software in terms of revenue, surpassing even the giant Microsoft. The most immediate benefit of having an online store is one relevant to its potential audience. An E-commerce site allows you to reach a number of potential clients, more than with any traditional business. An E-commerce site materializes the dream of any seller: sell anywhere, anytime and to anyone! Everyone with a computer or a smartphone and an internet connection will be, potentially, your client. You do not need to pay rent or to hire employees to receive customers.

In the phase of drafting your business plan, you will need to well define the scope behind your online store:

• Identify the product you want to sell: large or small, expensive or cheap. Selecting a good niche where you want to settle in will help you in the following endeavors.

• Choose the domain name carefully: because the final part is always .com or .net, the first part will be the one that will make you different from the others[7].

---

[7] On 123-reg.co.uk, GoDaddy.com, or Sedo.com, you can. They cost about ten euros, and if you are smart enough to find free domains that have potential for a commercial value domain that is particularly well-chosen, you can sell it also for thousands of euros.
I remember few years ago, when the domain VacationRentals.com was sold for $35,000.000. Of course, it is very difficult to get a strike like that, but you can still pull up a good bet by investing a bit of time in research.

Circled Money

Thoughts on Economy and Business, Trading and Personal Finance

Take care that the name that you choose is in some way related to the products you sell.

• Buy a web hosting service. The hosting is the virtual space that hosts your website, making it available on the network and accessible by web users around the world.

• Take care of the content and graphics of your site: they will be the "home" of your business. The web site design is what encourages buyers to stay and shop. Remember to include, in addition to the shopping cart and the product data sheets regulating the activities of the sale, your contact (possibly via telephone) and links to your social media pages and newsletter subscription.

• Get a "CMS e-Commerce". This is the software that allows buyers to browse the categories of the products you have for sale and create their shopping cart of those products that they want to purchase. Many of these software features include additional opportunities to control the availability of products in stock, create shipping documents and bills or calculate taxes. The most popular are Magento and Prestashop (an "all in one" program is less customizable, but easier to activate).

Shopify, Bigcommerce, Shopping Cart Elite and Volusio offer E-commerce sites that are pretty much already ready, for the payment of a monthly fee.

To avoid confusion about the offers available, you should make sure that, in addition to understanding all aspects of creating and maintaining an E-Commerce site, the E-Commerce software also allows you to have:

• Safe and secure diversified payments (credit cards, PayPal and eChecks); maximum protection of data privacy of your customers; and the ability to integrate sales with other sites like Amazon and Ebay.

• A schedule of marketing actions. All of the companies seeing E-commerce success have a strategy to attract customers. Among the most used marketing actions, it is useful to mention the search engine optimization (SEO), pay per click, and social campaigns on the main social media sites.

Circled Money
Thoughts on Economy and Business, Trading and Personal Finance

1.2. FOURTH ECONOMIC REVOLUTION: THE COGNITIVE SYSTEMS

1.2.1. Transcendence

Have you ever seen the movie Transcendence? I watched it on a flight going to Miami, and I was impressed about how the theme of the divine concepts of ubiquity and the almighty were matched to the technology and the absolute knowledge.

It talks about an inexhaustible virtual learning system with exponential growth in all directions, starting from the access to all channels of information, till the point where it takes, thanks to its knowledge, the full control of the matter deep to its primary elements.

A machine that improves by learning: this is the fourth revolution.

There is still no exhaustive definition of the industry 4.0 phenomenon, but in a nutshell, it can be described as the process that will lead to automated and interconnected industrial production.

These new digital technologies will have a profound impact to the world economic system and will deploy over four lines of development:

- The use of data, computing power and connectivity, big data, open data, the Internet of Things[8], machine-to-machine, and cloud computing for the centralization of information and its conservation.
- Data analytics: once the data are collected, they have to be managed to produce value. Today only 1% of data collected is used by enterprises that may get benefits from learning machines which improve by "learning" from the data collected and analyzed.
- Man-machine interface, which involves "touch" interfaces and augmented reality.
- The transition from digital to "real": additive manufacturing, 3D printing, robotics, communications, interactions, machine-to-machine, and using new technology to store and use energy in a targeted manner, streamlining costs and optimizing performances.

Now that computing power for the understanding, contextualizing, and linking data to "give meaning" to information is no longer the

---

[8] The Internet of Things is a huge market that, by 2020, at the global level, will reach 1.7 trillion dollars in products and services.

Circled Money

Thoughts on Economy and Business, Trading and Personal Finance

primary challenge, the current technologies, more than that fast and powerful, need to be more intelligent.

We are now ready to enter a new ecosystem of devices with artificial intelligence: a world where machines learn from machines, from self-driving cars to advanced services that require the recognition of images, video and language.

The higher computing capacity of the computers in fact helped save learning time; this allowed for the rise of new applications, from processing images (examples are the Prism and Artisto) to learning and predictive systems.

When I received my first computer, a Commodore-64, in the early 80s, I was so excited on the potential of this big keyboard that I thought to the possibility to run it to execute my primary school home works.

I imagined the task of describing a weekend up to the mountains, and in my naivety, I imaged the inputs I could have given.

Let's see:

- I wanted to describe a playground where I played soccer
- I wanted to have some spread of yellow and red flowers
- I was running and playing with my brother

I do not even know if, with these three simple inputs, a top advanced machine could better elaborate than a human mind, even today. At that time, I realized that I was missing the procedure of feeding the machine with these inputs, but I was really convinced that it was possible.

When I tried to explain how such a machine could have worked, my father threatened: "Do not even try to do that!".

Disappointingly, I soon discovered that my computer was not the magic tool that I was hoping for, but was a simple executor of the language BASIC using "IF and THEN", instructions that I used to copy from the instructions manual.

1.2.2. Cognitive Systems: Non-Thinking but Interpreting Machines

Google Play Music is an assistant based on artificial intelligence and machine learning that, based on weather conditions, our geographical location, the activities we are doing, and to what is (arguably) our state of mind, suggests music to listen to.

So, if we are in the office on a rainy Monday in October, the machine learning of "Big G" will propose specific music to pump up our mood. If, instead, we are in the gym, the assistant will

Circled Money

Thoughts on Economy and Business, Trading and Personal Finance

suggest something that can give us the right charge while we run on the tapis-roulant.

During a flight, or during an excursion on the Alps, Google Play Music works the same, using a play list that can also go offline. There will still be an assistant to suggest what music we can listen to, but it will be based on what we have heard recently. It's a good idea, especially for those who forget to load music directly into their smartphone's memory.

This is an example of cognitive systems that allow the processing and unstructured information management.

They process data in real time as it is analyzed, learning from past experiences about how to deal with specific situations and speed up the user's decision-making process, suggesting one or more possible solutions.

Others simulate the human ability to read and understand language in depth through artificial intelligence algorithms that does it in ways similar to human thinking

Some are based on language's map by means of a semantic network composed of a rich set of ontologies which contains millions of definitions and relationships between concepts.

For example they remove ambiguities and identify the proper meaning of words and expressions based on their contexts as well as the relationships between different concepts.

They absorb new knowledge from human experts, drawing from written texts as well as jargon, slang, word games, and other nuances of language.

Their applicability could cover a vast range of fields, from security and intelligence (with a dynamic control, as opposed to mere video-controlling or border defenses) to the development of relationships with customers by enhancing the decision-making processes for social analytic, knowledge management, compliance and many others.

1.2.3. Flash-Crash

London 06102016 - someone called it "fat finger" .

I remember once one of my colleagues, a big German guy of 120 kilos, that was struggling in typing the right letter every time he used the keyboard to write an email or a text, especially when he was in hurry. That was an example of fat finger.

On the 6th October 2016, the trading room robots executed the wrong order to sell (the "fat finger," typing the wrong keys) after having misinterpreted the statements of French president Francois

Circled Money

Thoughts on Economy and Business, Trading and Personal Finance

Hollande. They are fingers, whether real or virtual, that fail by physically or virtually touching the wrong button which triggers the collapse of markets. It happened to the pound, which plummeted in Asian markets by 6.1% in few moments on the heels of sales that they crushed to values never before seen since decades.

According to market experts, the attack on the pound could have been driven by the hyper-sensitivity of an algorithm that was automatically activated by processing the comments reported by The Financial Times and attributed to President François Hollande on Brexit.

In other words, the flash crash would have been caused by the hasty interpretation of the words of the French Prime Minister, which were "translated" into an encouragement for massive sales. The bounce came two minutes later, and this confirms the theory of the error in the trading rooms or, at least, the non-voluntarism.

To further explain the sudden collapse, then there is its timing: it happened a little after 1,00 am (GMT), when volumes of trade are at the minimum, when America's trading sessions have just finished their day and the Asian ones are about to start.

"London has decided to proceed on the path of Brexit. And I think it will be a hard Brexit."

The Financial Times posted online this comment from Holland at 7.07 Singapore time which caused a vertical drop of 120 seconds' duration. The pound collapsed and hit 6.1% loss, passing from 1.26 on the dollar up to 1.18 after brushing 1,14.

Thanks also to the poor liquidity at that time of the day (a few hours after the Wall Street market closure and right before the opening times of the AUX50 in Australia), operators buying pounds were cut off by the immediate drop caused by the news, which triggered the execution of stop loss orders at 1,236. Like a rolling snowball, these automatic sales signaled to "shorters" (those investing on a the pound drop) to sell pounds in order to earn. When the exchange rate touched 1,14, those that before wanted the pound to go down started buying pounds again with the expectation now that British currency could raise again ("longers").

When these signals to buy at 1,14 were executed, the exchange rate rebounded, pushing the same HFT (High Frequency Trading) system into a buying phase and making the operators earn again.

HFT is a form of market intervention that uses sophisticated software (and sometimes, also, hardware) tools driven by mathematical algorithms, which act on markets with the purpose of profiting from extremely low margins (with oscillations in the

Circled Money

Thoughts on Economy and Business, Trading and Personal Finance

space of milliseconds). Being these margins of the order of cents of Euro, Dollar or whatever, the HFT must act on large amounts (thousands, or tens of thousands, of times per day). According to recent estimates the automatic trading manages in the USA about 60% of share exchanges.

By using automatic algorithms for the analysis and prediction of data coming from the markets and following sell/buy instructions, these trading strategies flood the market with huge amounts of "execute immediately" or "cancel" orders.

This "Status of the Market" is created only to test market conditions: because of the very short latency times, they may not lead to transactions. In this way, the software collects information with which it builds market maps, on the basis of which actual transactions are directed and designed to perform in short time. For example: it may happen that a traditional investor, looking at the order book of a shares (the list of waiting and selling orders at not marketable prices), thinks that the same share is easily exchangeable. Instead, in the moment in which the HFT decides to eventually retire, as if by magic, the book is "empty"; the market becomes illiquid. With that, all of the operators will remain "stuck" in their positions, as there are no sellers able to liquidate the assets; if they want to sell, they are forced to do it at a lower prices, or buyers that want to enter long in the market and who have to buy at a higher price [9].

At the base of the investment strategy of a robot, in most cases, there is the following logical structure: "If something happens......, then buy (or sell)." The automatic trader first analyzes, for example the trend of a stock price in a given period of time (i.e. 10 years), then, after having identified the significant values, it compares them with other variables (which are always traced back to numbers). At the end based on a statistical analysis, the system releases a forecast that says: "If the title exceeds 10 euros, then buy". This description, of course, is a simplification to say that the mechanism considers the shares (and all other financial assets) in the same way as simple numbers.

This dynamic "dirties" the informational value of the formation of a share's price. In the moment in which the percentage share of

---

[9] Example of an Order Book

Buyers - Ask			Sellers - Bid		
Trader	Volume	Price (€)	Price (€)	Volume	Trader
Sam	150	16.70	16.72	200	Bob
Tom	100	16.69	16.73	300	Tim
Brad	500	16.68	16.74	200	Mark
Tim	200	16.67	16.75	800	Ben

Circled Money

Thoughts on Economy and Business, Trading and Personal Finance

trade handled by the algorithms is high, strategies and quantitative references coming from these trading systems become, themselves, the market's reference, based on statistical concepts and automatic processes and not on the real values of a company share for example.

In this way, the statement that "all information is reflected in the prices", which is the fundamental principle of the perfect competition, loses great part of its meaning, and the market becomes an easy winning arena for those who can rely on the most effective, advanced, and expensive technology tools.

2. SECTION TWO: A FINANCIAL INFRASTRUCTURE

2.1. THE BANK

I have always had a positive attitude towards the banks, perhaps also because my father was a bank employee and the wellness of our family was always backed by his work.

Beside this, historically the bank has always held a primary role in society. Just think about western movies and imagine the bank next to the saloon and the sheriff's office on the main street of those dusty villages. Initially the bank served primarily to secure workers' salary deposits, then it evolved to an entity allowed to lend money and then, gradually, it entered more and more complex business inter-mediations, including providing contractual performance guarantees or access to advanced platforms for financial products trading.

Facilitating and securing the exchange of money the financing system also helped to make business activities more attractive simply because entrepreneurs, better focused on 'objective activity', without the problem of collecting capital assets, could develop new ideas and grow. Furthermore, the assessment of a project for which the funding was requested helped to define its business case

Circled Money

Thoughts on Economy and Business, Trading and Personal Finance

and the strength of the idea and to become better aware of its potentials and expectations.

With the banks, we invented the safe deposit box, armored glasses, metal detectors, magnetic cards, developed secure transactions, and created the most advanced levels of software reliability. The ties on white shirts, the good manners and the professionalism and reliability of the people behind the cash-desks created a symbol of trust for handling our money. They also played a role towards a more equal distribution of wealth by extending the ability to hold assets like cars, mobile phones and air conditioners: items that would have otherwise been offered only to a limited number of people. A healthy banking system paves the way to safe investments, encouraging private lending rather than just spending or saving without purpose. The banks foster efficient business activities and cut those that are not profitable, feeding competitiveness and innovation, the propensity to take risks, and its management. They have legalized a credit system that otherwise would have been prey to usury rather than providing direct employment to millions of people and moving the wheel of the progress for the whole mankind. Despite that, my experience drove me to no longer believe in the utility of their advisory services for two main reasons: an inability to build and understand specific and personal customer demands, and to detach from an inherent conflict of interest. Beside the second topic, the main problem is that while in the past there was a huge difference of financial awareness between customer and consultant, today even if there are still wide margins for improvements, the gap between these two stakeholder is strongly reduced as well as the added value of that service. With the tools and so easy access to markets, I do not see why we shouldn't be able to manage our money on our own. With a reasonable level of knowledge about the markets, their financial products, and our personality, we could define at the best what our targets are and our risk tolerance. The banks will still support our activities with their internet based technology and the required warranties for our transactions, in addition to providing real-time data and database statistics. And, of course, they will still provide money that we can reinvest in a profitable way:

Circled Money

Thoughts on Economy and Business, Trading and Personal Finance

Two examples:

Tom	Sam
Buys 1 house with $100,000 cash without mortgage	Buys 5 houses with $20,000 cash payment each and total $400,000 mortgage
Revenue per month : $1,000 Cost for Interests : 0 Net Profit : $1,000	Revenue per month : $5,000 Cost for Interests : $2,000 Net Profit : $3,000
Total revenue after 5 years : $60,000	Total revenue after 5 years : $300,000
Total net profit after 5 years : $60,000	Total net profit after 5 years : $180,000
Profit from house sale : $50,000	Profit from 5 house sales : $250,000
Total Profit : $60,000+$50,000 = $110,000	Total Profit : $180,000+$250,000 = $430,000

2.2. THE CIRCLE : WORK REVENUE AND CAPITAL REVENUE

As we will see in the next chapters, the total revenue of an individual is composed by a portion of revenue coming from his labor activity and a portion of revenue coming from his capital asset. The financial institutions have the power to make the world swinging between the different level of combinations of labor and capital intensity: in theory for a high value of capital yield, the revenue from labor could not justify the effort to work for it.

In practice, what happens is that for high values of capital returns can be more cost effective to not work, and then, for those that can afford it, have the capital asset working, by means of real estate or entrepreneurial or financial investments. On the long terms, we are back to what I call the Circle: the work income progressively decreases and the production and investment profitability also plunge, making the capital income less attractive and revamping the work income. With the work income becoming attractive again, the new growing production activity foster new capital investments and so on.

The Capital absolves therefore two main alternate functions:

- value reserve (i.e. food stock, cash deposits, financial products etc.), in favorable capital income phases and
- production catalyst (for machines, plants, buildings, etc.), in favorable work income times.

2.3. FIRST FUNDAMENTAL LAW OF CAPITALISM[10]

Assets (Total): These are financial assets (cash, or the market value of financial investments) and non-financial assets (i.e. the market value of Real Estate, Land, and Infrastructure - but also non-tangible assets such as patents) both less liabilities (less debts and loans).

Income (Total): This is the result of a yearly in/out flow of salaries, profits, interests, dividends, and rental fees, and therefore the result of Work Income + Assets Income.

From these two main definitions we introduce Beta and Alpha as follows:

Beta = Asset/Income

Alpha (The Portion Of Income From Asset Income) = Asset income / Income

R (Yield Rate From Asset) = Assets Income / Assets

and therefore:

Alpha x Income = R x Assets

From which we derive the First Fundamental Law of Capitalism:

Alpha = Beta x R

---

[10] Capital in the Twenty-First Century (2013), Thomas Piketty

Or

Beta = Alpha / R

And

R = Alpha/Beta

This is the relationship between Yield Rate From Asset (R) and Beta (the ratio between Asset and Income)

For the next topic however we will consider another aspect of this relation and we will introduce a new concept.

The relationship between the variations of Yield rates from Asset (R) and variations of Beta is ruled by the Production's Function.

The Production's Function is a mathematical formula that allows one to summarize the state of technologies applicable in a given business environment, describing the relationship between the amounts of various factors of production (input) to be used and the level of productivity (output). By adopting the technological innovations made possible by technical-scientific progress (assuming that progress increases the productivity and the efficiency of production facilities), the function of production displayed as Y' moves by vertical translation.

Circled Money

Thoughts on Economy and Business, Trading and Personal Finance

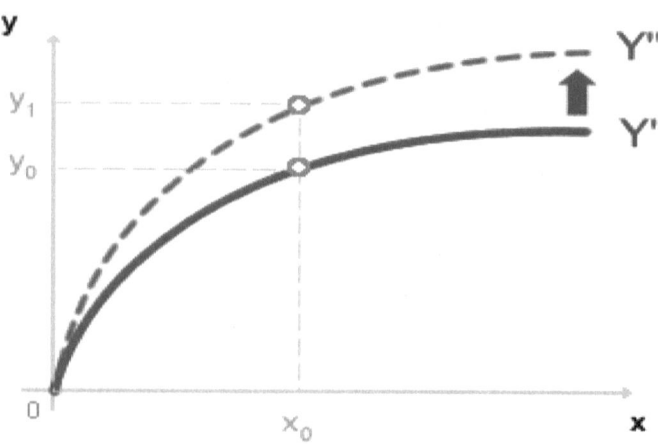

Technological innovations allow for increasing the level of production, making the same use of other factors, or lowering consumption of other production factors to produce the same quantity of a product (production efficiency). The production function is the maximum product obtainable from different combinations of productive factors, or **Q=F(L;K)** where L denotes the amount of labor used in production, K denotes the quantity of capital asset and Q the amount of output [11].

---

[11] **Cobb-Douglas** formula

Capital asset and Labor are the two production elements (inputs) that, put in a production process, generate the final product (output). How the variation of the Capital asset and Labor affect the result of the function of production is explained with the concept of the elasticity of substitution between capital and labor. In other words, this principle gives an indication as to the possibility of replacing capital with labor or labor with capital in order to produce the requested goods and services. We will not go into the details of the two extreme cases of elasticity in Production [12], because what is important to this thread is the principle of marginal productivity that gives a measure of the

---

[12] A function of production with zero elasticity is a function of production with fixed coefficients. By increasing one between Labor or Capital, the marginal productivity is null.

If, for example, our production is the assembly operation of 1 steering wheel and 4 tires per one car, then if we use 2 steering wheels, we will not increase the car's production rate. In this case, the proportion between the two elements of the function of production is fixed.

A function of production with infinite elasticity is a function where marginal productivity is proportionally increased(or decreased) with the variation of the two elements of the production function.

If, for example, we take the case of a function of production for the aircraft system integration portrayed in section two of the 2nd economic revolution, we can think, in theory, about replacing capital (outsourcing) and labor (internal engineering resource) in full independency without changing the level of production.

Circled Money

Thoughts on Economy and Business, Trading and Personal Finance

increases of productivity against the marginal increment of one factor[13].

13

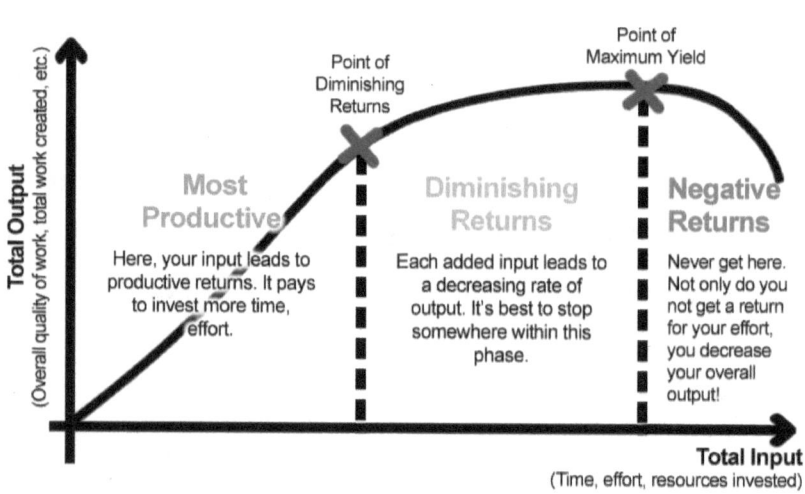

https://personalexcellence.co/blog/law-of-diminishing-returns/

Marginal productivity also depends on the specific environment and its boundary conditions. It is positive when the deployment of one of the factors implies an increase in production and the opposite when it is negative (the additional deployment of resources generates a reduction of production). We may find ourselves in a situation where, in a factory production line, an additional worker has no positive effect on output (it might even be negative, if the physical installation space is restricted). Also with regard to consumer preferences, the following illustrative example can explain the concept: for a thirsty individual, the first glass of water is very desirable and therefore affords a high benefit. The second glass will bring satisfaction. From the third glass on, every next dose will be less satisfying until you get to the **point of creating nuisance** by suggesting it. Therefore, repeated doses (units) of a given item descend in consumer interest. Do you remember the case of the 4 cathodic ray tubes TV's in 3 rooms apartment?

Based on the simplest economic models, in a perfect competition on capital and labor markets, the portion of profitability from capital (or assets) equals the marginal productivity of the capital (and, therefore, the additional contribution of a unit of capital to the specific production environment).

2.4. SECOND FUNDAMENTAL LAW OF CAPITALISM[14]

S (Savings rate): defined as the percentage that can be saved from your annual income.

G (Growth rate): defined as the percentage growth of our annual income (for example, that which is linked to inflation).

The Second Law of Capitalism is defined as :

S/G = Beta

with

Beta = Alpha / R = Asset/Income

We can also say that :

G (Growth Rate, of labor income) = S (Savings Rate) x R (Yield from Asset) / Alpha (Portion of Income from Asset Income),

or

G (Growth Rate) = S (Savings Rate) x Income (Total) / Asset,

from which, since R is Yield from Asset (Marginal Productivity), then

R = Alpha x Income /Asset = Alpha / Beta

or

---

[14] Capital in the Twenty-First Century (2013), Thomas Piketty

R = Alpha x G/S

or

Alpha = R x S / G

The relationship between the rate of savings (S) and the growth rate (G) indicates my long-term capacity to accumulate capital, or the number of years of income that can be accumulated in the form of capital asset.

The above formula can be read in different ways.

Here are some examples:

The Portion of Income from Asset Income (Alpha) increases if R (Capital Profitability) grows and decreases if G (the Growth Rate of Labor Income) increases. The same if S grows.

Unless R decreased, Alpha increases if: S > G.

Capital Profitability (R) decreases when the portion of income from Capital Assets (ALPHA) decreases more than how the ratio between Savings Rate (S) / Growth Rate (G) increases.

Capital Profitability (R) decreases when the portion of income from Capital Assets (ALPHA) decreases more than how much the ratio between Capital/Income increases

If R is fixed, then the portion of income from Capital Income increases if S increases or G decreases, which make us think of the

Circled Money

Thoughts on Economy and Business, Trading and Personal Finance

salary abatement given by a robotic economy (where production is only pursued with capital and no human labor).

If at the end of XXI century for the world we have $G = 1\%$ e $S = 10\%$, then for $R = 5\%$, Alpha would be 50%; half of the income comes from capital income.

In order to establish our capital profitability target (that will be needed to asses risk and investments), it is important to understand the increase rate of our marginal productivity of capital and the increase of capital stock. One of the target that we will set in the third section is the understanding of the level of increase of profitability when we increase the financial exposure of our investment.

If, for example, we have the availability of an additional asset of 100 euro (in cash, equipment or land) that enables us to increase the level of production of products, food or cash of 5 euro per year, we have the marginal productivity of 5 euro over 100, which means 5%.

It is also obvious that the marginal productivity changes depends on the initial capital stock. In fact, the higher the capital stock, the less is the marginal utility that come from a capital investment increase, which brings us to the paradox that too much capital kills capital.

For example, if each landowner already has thousands of hectares to work, it is likely that the additional yield resulting from an additional hectare more is negligible.

So if a country has already built an extraordinary number of dwellings for which each inhabitant can live in hundreds of square meters, then an increase of wellness procured by extra property or in more than one square meter in an apartment building of 400 square meters is minimal. The same goes for production machinery and capital.

2.5. A FAMILY BUSINESS PLAN

In this paragraph, we will propose a method of analyzing our own financial structure, working with figures and orders of magnitude that reflect the average status of wealth in the most advanced Western Europe countries. In that way, we will find numbers and monetary references that can be easily fitted to our own situation.

In countries like Italy, the average Beta value equals 6 (600%).

We can, therefore, think that, for a family income of 30'000 euro per year, we own a total equity of 180'000 euro (excluding debts) which are statistically split into 90'000 Euro in non-financial assets (real estate) and 90'000 Euro in financial assets (bank accounts, shares and similar).

Circled Money

Thoughts on Economy and Business, Trading and Personal Finance

Being the total income compounded by work income and financial income we can say that for a financial income of 5% per year (the average yield from an asset), the portion of financial income over the total income is 30% (9'000 Euro).

The portion of financial income over total income (Alpha) is given by Beta x R (capital yield) = 6 x 5% is 30%.

This gives us an indication on how to set our financial goals (in this case be aligned with the average), and the right method for managing our equities.

For the 90'000 euro in Real Estate Assets (either we use it as our own living place, or we rent it) the 5% a year equals to 4'500 euro (375 euro per month x 12)

For the 90'000 in financial assets the 4'500 euro will come from a reasonable investment of a shares with the ratio price/dividend of 18 [15]. Therefore, if Alpha is 30% then Work Income is 70%.

The same principles apply to a national economic system or generic enterprise, and it is from the latter that we borrow classic accounting tools and principles (the balance sheet and the cash flow statement) to run our exercise.

---

[15] This equals 18 years to recover the investment; which means 5% = 4500 Euro

We decide to study a case of financial infrastructure of a middle-class 2016 Italian family, with a financial status which I consider to be solid:
1. 40-year-old parents, married in 2003, with university degree
2. 2 children
3. No inherited assets
4. An initial asset of 10'000 Euro in 2003
5. Working since 2003
6. A cumulative salary of 90'000 euros gross per annum
7. An annual savings from 2003 of 2000 euros per month for the first 6 years of marriage, 1500 for the second 6 years. and 1000 after 12 years
8. Savings invested in financial instruments and real estate
9. 1 apartment bought in 2009, after 6 years, as own residence
10. The second apartment bought for investment after 12 years, given for rental at 5% per annum of the value of the property
11. Both of the apartments purchased with mortgage loans of 25 year terms for 70% of their value (a total of 180'000)
12. About 20% of financial losses from the financial crisis of 2008-2016
13. About a 20% loss of real estate value
14. 2 leased cars

Circled Money

Thoughts on Economy and Business, Trading and Personal Finance

15. 1 loan for consumer credit
16. A medium standard of living, no excesses, and a rational approach (2 Saturdays per month dinner out in restaurants, two Sundays per month for a day out, and 2 longer holidays per year: Christmas and Summer)

Nicola Matarese

Balance Sheet			2016	NOTES
Assets				
	Current Assets			
		Cash reserve	25'000	Savings plus Revenues from shares, work & RE assets
		Investement Funds	30'000	Selling value of funds at row R
		Market Shares	25'000	Selling value of shares at row S
		Total current assets	**80'000**	
	Fixed (Long-Term) Assets			
		Property, plant, and equipment	260'000	market selling value of real estate
		Durable goods	20'000	furniture and others
		Total fixed assets	**280'000**	
Total Assets			**360'000**	
Liabilities				
	Liabilities			
		Short-term loan 1	5'000	2 years liabilities - consumer credit repayment
		Short-term loan 2	30'000	5 years liabilities - car leasing
		Long-term debt	250'000	Mortgages : 25 years liabilities
		Total Liabilities	**285'000**	
Net Asset			**75'000**	Total Asset - Total Liabilities
Total Investments				
		Funds	55'000	invested savings + all losses - all gains
		Shares	40'000	invested savings + all losses - all gains
		Cash	10'000	Initial asset + Retained Earnings
		Flat 1	80'000	purchasing cost - mortgage
		Flat 2	75'000	purchasing cost - mortgage
		Total Investments	**260'000**	
GAIN / LOSS			**-185'000**	Net Asset - Equity

Circled Money

Thoughts on Economy and Business, Trading and Personal Finance

Income Statement

Income		2016	% On Total Revenue	NOTES
	Shares Sales net Revenue Consolidated	2'500		Asset Income
	Flat Rentals Revenue	7'200		Asset Income
	Salary 1	50'000		Work income
	Salary 2	38'000		Work income
	Total Income	**97'700**		
Operating Expenses				
	Salary Income taxes	38'720	40%	44% Salary incomes
	Food	7'200	7%	600 x month
	Education	1'000	1%	school & books
	Car leasing 1	3'600	4%	300 x month
	Car leasing 2	2'400	2%	200 x month
	Fuel	1'200	1%	100 x month - 1000 km x month
	Insurances	1'800	2%	150 x month
	Own Flat Mortgage	5'280	5%	440 x month
	Rented Flat Mortgage	4'536	5%	378 x month
	RE Income taxes	1'512	2%	21% income taxes
	RE Property taxes	6'000	6%	Property taxes x 2 flats
	RE expenses / maintenance	1'800	2%	900 a year x 2 flats
	Home consumptions (electricity, heating)	600	1%	50 a month
	Leisures (restaurant, gifts, personal care)	3'000	3%	250 a month
	Holidays (Christmas and Summer)	3'000	3%	flight tickets + car expenses
	Utilities (clothes, furniture, home appliances)	2'400	2%	200 a month
	Total operating expenses	**84'048**	**86%**	
Net Income YEARLY (savings)		13'652	14%	
Net Income MONTHLY (savings)		1'138		

Nicola Matarese

25 years business plan

Age Children	Age Parents	Year	Liabilities	Total asset	Net asset	Equity (Cumulative Savings)	Loss/Gain (net asset - equity)	Notes	cum savings (1% yearly increase)
-	40	2016	285'000	360'000	75'000	260'000	-185'000		13'652
1	41	2017	266'500	373'652	107'152	273'652	-166'500		27'441
2	42	2018	248'000	387'304	139'304	287'441	-148'137		41'229
3	43	2019	232'000	400'956	168'956	301'229	-132'273		55'018
4	44	2020	216'000	414'608	198'608	315'018	-116'410		68'806
5	45	2021	200'000	428'260	228'260	328'806	-100'546		82'595
6	46	2022	190'000	441'912	251'912	342'595	-90'683		96'383
7	47	2023	180'000	455'564	275'564	356'383	-80'819		110'172
8	48	2024	170'000	469'216	299'216	370'172	-70'956		123'960
9	49	2025	160'000	482'868	322'868	383'960	-61'092		137'749
10	50	2026	150'000	496'520	346'520	397'749	-51'229	Children Expenses increase	145'537
11	51	2027	140'000	510'172	370'172	405'537	-35'365	Children Expenses increase	153'326
12	52	2028	130'000	523'824	393'824	413'326	-19'502	Children Expenses increase	161'114
13	53	2029	120'000	537'476	417'476	421'114	-3'638	Children Expenses increase	168'903
14	54	2030	110'000	551'128	441'128	428'903	12'225	Children Expenses increase	176'691
15	55	2031	100'000	564'780	464'780	436'691	28'089	Children Expenses increase	184'480
16	56	2032	90'000	578'432	488'432	444'480	43'952	Children Expenses increase	192'268
17	57	2033	80'000	592'084	512'084	452'268	59'816	Children Expenses increase	200'057
18	58	2034	70'000	605'736	535'736	460'057	75'679	Children Advanced Study Expenses	201'845
19	59	2035	60'000	619'388	559'388	461'845	97'543	Children Advanced Study Expenses	203'634
20	60	2036	50'000	633'040	583'040	463'634	119'406	Children Advanced Study Expenses	205'422
21	61	2037	40'000	646'692	606'692	465'422	141'270	Children Advanced Study Expenses	207'211
22	62	2038	30'000	660'344	630'344	467'211	163'133	Children Advanced Study Expenses	208'999
23	63	2039	20'000	673'996	653'996	468'999	184'997	Children Advanced Study Expenses	210'788
24	64	2040	10'000	687'648	677'648	470'788	206'860	Children Advanced Study Expenses	212'576
25	65	2041	-	701'300	701'300	472'576	228'724	Children Advanced Study Expenses	214'365

Circled Money

Thoughts on Economy and Business, Trading and Personal Finance

Also displayed in the following trend lines:

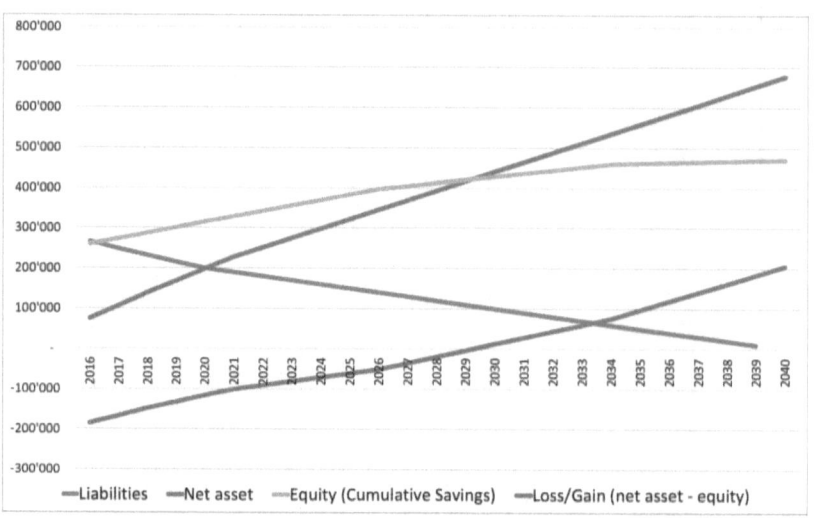

With a report of that kind, in addition to having a better control over our financial structure, we can plan long-term projects with a deeper and better awareness of our financial targets, prepare our investments in advance, make a saving plan for our children's university, plan where to live once we're retired, and beat our financial goals.

Let's try to build a performance measuring tool of the model with the definitions given under the chapters of the First and Second Law of Capitalism:

2016 PERFORMANCE INDEXES			
DATA INPUTS		DATA OUTPUTS	
Growth	3.93%	Financial Asset / Property Asset	28.57%
Asset	360'000	Cash Availability / Financial Investment	31.25%
Income	97'700	Alfa (portion of income from assets)	-0.42%
Yearly Savings	13'652	Beta	3.68
Financial Asset	80'000	R (Profitability of Assets - Marginal Productivity)	-0.11%
Property Asset	280'000	Saving Rate	13.97%
Asset Income (Net)	-248	Beta limit	3.56
Total Income (Net)	58'980		

2016 FAMILY ASSETS PERFORMANCE INDEXES			
FINANCIAL ASSETS			
Financial Income	2'500		
Financial Investment	95'000	ROI - Financial Income/ Financial Investment	2.63%

REAL ESTATE ASSETS – RENTED FLAT			
Real Estate income (Net)	-2'748		
Real Estate investment (own capital plus mortgage)	165'000	ROI - Real Estate Income/ Real Estate Investment (own capital plus mortgage)	-1.67%
Real Estate Investments (own capital only)	75'000	ROI - Real Estate Income/ Real Estate Investment (own capital only)	-3.66%

Using these numbers, we can make two considerations. For financial assets, an annual fixed performance of 2.5% gain a year

Circled Money

Thoughts on Economy and Business, Trading and Personal Finance

(also called marginal productivity, quotes of capital profitability, or yield from Assets) is overall not really exciting but, as long as inflation remains below 2.5%, it could be considered a good performance. For real estate assets, we need to go a bit deeper.

Even the yearly profitability is negative, we need to consider the re-evaluation of the property over the years and the cancellation of the hypothec at the end of the mortgage period. With a property re-valuation which can be reasonably estimated to be the same as the inflation index, we try to formulate some hypotheses (using no revaluation on rental fees and no increase in taxes and expenses, but only property value) and get the following :

	RENTED FLAT	
A	cost for mortgage, maintenance and taxes less revenue from rental fee per year	-2'748
B	cost of investment inclusive of 75'000 Euro for initial investment till the mortgage is repaid (from year 2016 to year 2040)	-140'952

C	Sale Value 2016	130'000
D	Sale Value 2040 (assumed 2% inflation-revaluation)	209'097

E	Gain (D-B)	68'145

Which, in 24 years, gives an annual average gain of 3,000 which, with over 75,000 of initial own capital investment, gives a ROI of 4%. Not bad, if we could really count on a 2% real estate escalation.

3. SECTION THREE: INVEST WITH PERSONALITY

3.1. GREED & FREEDOM

3.1.1. The beginning of the dream

If it is true that the market is (as I think) in all effects a natural system, when we decide to enter the financial investments world, we need to discover our natural way to interact with it.

It's amazing how free I feel at home in the evening when I am studying the opportunity in the market session for the next day and loading my system of tens of buy and sell order. It's only me and the screen, an array of numbers, price trends lines and news as well as the hope that my theories, interpretations, methods and experience drive me to set the right strategy. I am not sure if it is a form of addiction, as well; but in all cases, what is absolutely exciting is the freedom and awareness that there is a possibility for me to have access to all the money of the world and there's even a remote possibility (albeit technically possible) of earning trillions of $ [16].

---

[16] All stock markets added together are worth $70 trillion. The notional value of the derivatives market is estimated to be $630 trillion.
The total of the world's physical currency – all coins and bills denominated in dollars, euros, yen, and other currencies – is about $5 trillion.

Circled Money

Thoughts on Economy and Business, Trading and Personal Finance

Also, which is very nice as well, since I do not do real-time trading, I have my money working themselves. "Off-line trading" allows us not to be affected by emotional aspects as well as not to waste time over the day, avoiding the temptation to look at the markets all times.

There is a say that admonish "Sell, gain and repent" which well describes the frustration of those traders that, operating in real-time, sell too early, losing the opportunity to ride the rising price trend.

The "off-line trading", will not erase that sensation but alleviates the pain, at least just because you see the results of the day at closed markets.

It all started in December of 2002 with my first little investments in mutual funds. They were the first years post 9/11, when stock exchanges were recovering from the losses of those tragic events and from the burst bubble of the dotcoms few years ahead. Right before the 2000, when the internet became a mass phenomenon,

---

All money market, savings and deposits total $80.9 trillion
Global wealth (as defined in section two) in 2016 is 256 trillion USD. It will be 334 trillion USD by 2021. The global debt is $199 trillion.

the stock markets changed as well, and "trading online" was the novelty buzzword[17].

In any case, thanks to internet and dotcoms, we have easy access to all markets. Globalization, with the explosion of China (with growth rate of 10% per year), drove me to buy 5,000 Euro in China's Shares Fund. However, that investment in mutual funds didn't give me the feeling of controlling my destiny and soon after, I turned to the stock market and ETF's.

Some rightfully believe that shares are not suitable to non-professional traders and that the stock market is for insiders. No matter how much you successfully analyze companies because executives, directors, and senior staff, including their friends and relatives, will always know more than us.

---

[17] There was a magazine named "Trading On-Line" which came out with very few issue numbers, but with some very interesting threads.
It spoke about neural networks and complex algorithms for trading, and even if I didn't have enough background to understand software code lines – also because they were copied and pasted on pages of a magazine - I was irresistibly attracted.
There was another article that tied in trading to horoscopes and constellations, which of course I didn't read - perhaps just because I always find it difficult to understand things about which I am skeptical in first case.
It's not that I am lazy, because I am always working (or at least, I always have always my brain turned on), but I have a natural tendency that leads me to take shortcuts to get the best acceptable results from the minimum effort. It's a matter of personality and saving energy.

Circled Money

Thoughts on Economy and Business, Trading and Personal Finance

Along with investment banks and those that have direct contacts with the companies there is a large group of people who have a clear advantage over all of us.

If we limit our assessment to this consideration, foreign exchange markets, commodities, bonds, and even CFDs are more like instruments that put all the players on the same ground.

On the other side, when we buy shares, we buy a piece of a productive organization made from human resources, assets, and buildings while other financial products are only the results of financial engineering operations, with conventional values registered on paper.

Therefore, while, with shares, we can identify a long-term trend with results based on factual evidence and real economy, the same is not true for other financial products. Just think about the fact that in a deal with shares, the seller and buyer can both win, as opposed to derivatives where for every winner, there is a loser.

3.1.2. Finance for Gravity

In the ascending phase of a share, in order for it to keep raising it is necessary that someone put new money in the market.

In descending phases, the dynamics are inverted: without money, the price is not supported and it plunges (as it is falling by gravity).

Let's suppose that a trader (who we will call trader S(eller)) initially purchased 100 shares at $10 per share, for a total of $1'000.

Now, in order for the share to reach an higher price, there will be a need for another trader B(uyer) who has the intention of buying the shares for an higher price.

If the price goes up to $1'100 as a result of this transaction, then trader B pays $100 more than what S paid.

The two independent variables of the price function are money and demand.

The first conclusion is that the price rises if there is an availability of money. If there is no money, the price will not increase, but the availability of money is not a guarantee that the prices will go up: if there is money availability but no demand for a specific share (when all those who were interested in buying have concluded their purchases), the price cannot rise.

To use a terminology from the mathematical theorems, money availability is a necessary but not sufficient condition for the price to rise. Like the money, the same applies for the demand.

Conversely, to make prices fall, there is no need to verify either of these two conditions (availability of money and demand).

Whatever trader B purchases for $1100 (if he has the money), he can get rid of for $900 easier. Therefore, while prices require money to move up, they don't to move down; this generally means that for the price, it is easier to plunge rather than climb or, in other words, prices can move down quicker than they came up[18].

Price gravity could be part of the explanation of why in the markets there is a proven asymmetrical instability : markets seem to be less unstable when they are growing, and more unstable when they are in decline.

3.1.3. Trading Volumes

Price and volume dynamics follow phases of accumulation (preceding positive trends) and distribution (preceding negative trends). From here, the cycle starts again.

It is important to know that supply and demand is "made" by strong hands; i.e. from institutional entities that are able to trade a significant portion of free-floating stocks (shares available in the market).

They define shares price trends by managing volumes of supply and demand, while mass investors (small and individual players),

---

[18] As another example of this tendency, just consider that two percentage displacements in opposite directions result in an absolute decrease.
1'000 + 5% - 5% = 997,5 or 1'000 − 5% + 5% = 997,5.

unless they trigger mass actions during circumstances related to extraordinary events, can have a limited influence to these price cycles.

The volumes represent the set of closed transactions of Bid and Asking price of a given financial instrument in a given unit of time, at a price that behaves as follows:

- when the demand (Ask) for a good exceeds supply (Bid), the prices go up
- when supply (Bid) exceeds demand (Ask), prices go down

The analysis of volume is used to recognize the stability and reliability of a movement, its strength, and therefore the likely evolution of prices.

This is certainly not an easy thing, and sometimes requires a sort of creativity and instinct, matured with experience and long observation in relation to price/volume ratios.

Saying that the volumes were high does not mean that someone has sold (or bought) a lot; but only that many "pieces" were sold (as many as, on the Ask side, were bought).

The general rules of interpreting signals from price/volume relationships are depicted in 3 rules:

Circled Money

Thoughts on Economy and Business, Trading and Personal Finance

Rule 1: Volumes confirm Trends

Trend	Volumes	Signal
Positive	Increasing	Buy
Positive	Decreasing	-
Negative	Increasing	Sell
Negative	Decreasing	-

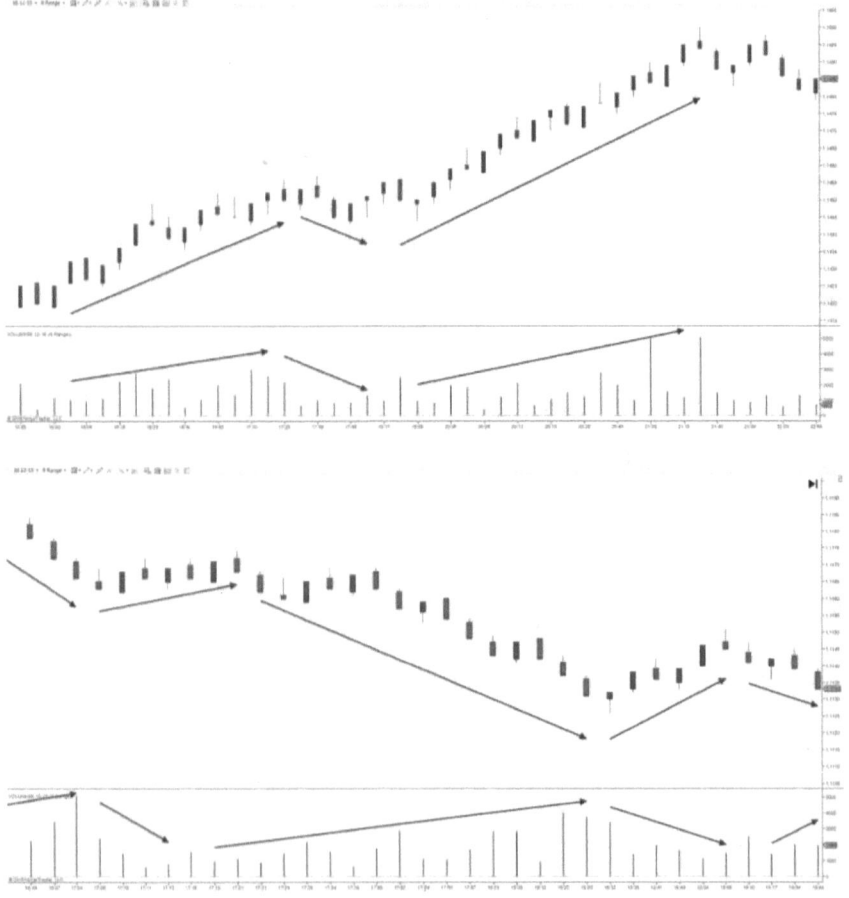

Rule 2. Trend Reliability

Trend	Volumes	Signal
Positive	Increasing	Trend Reliable
Positive	Decreasing	Trend Not Reliable
Negative	Increasing	Trend Reliable
Negative	Decreasing	Trend Not Reliable

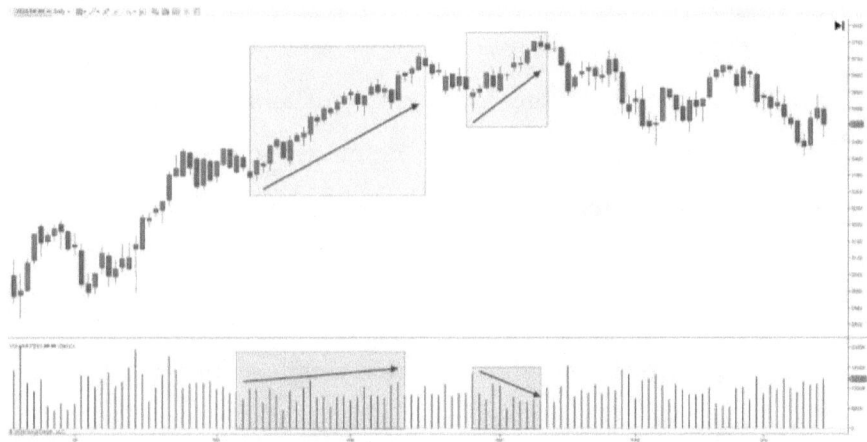

Circled Money

Thoughts on Economy and Business, Trading and Personal Finance

Rule 3. Inverted Trends

a) Volumes Decreasing in Proximity of a Maximum

In practice, when after a long or strong positive trend the volume decreases as a result of a lack of demand, we can expect a down-trend reversal.

b) Volumes Increasing in Proximity of a Minimum

Conversely, when after a long or strong negative trend the volume increases, we can expect an up-trend reversal

c) Peak Volumes in Proximity of a Maximum

If, at the end of a positive trend, prices remain basically stable but the volumes increases significantly, we can expect that there is a strong distribution.

d) Peak Volumes in Proximity of a Minimum

At the end of a negative trend, prices remain basically stable; but the volumes grow significantly. This divergence of price/volume indicates accumulation and predicts a phase reversal to the upside.

In conclusion:

Case	Trend	Volumes	Signal
a	Positive over Maximum	Decreasing	Sell
b	Negative over Minimum	Increasing	Buy
c	End Positive Trend– Stable Prices	High	Sell
d	End Negative Trend - Stable Prices	High	Buy

3.2. STRATEGY.

3.2.1. Observation

Shares research and selection criteria based on company financial fundamentals (fundamental analysis) is a valid concept, but holds some cautions: financial data can be misleading and not really clear for home traders, and either they are positive or negative, they always come after the facts (information is usually released on a quarterly basis). As a consequence of this, the market reaction to this inputs is difficult to predict. Technical analysis, compared to the fundamental analysis, gives us inputs for managing information (prices and volumes) coming straight from the market and operates with a variable spectrum of time frames from months to minute-by-minute (or tick to tick). According to this technique, the news has no importance at the end: what matters (and sets the price) is the reaction to news. News may affect values of the listed companies, but the price is not the value; the price is only the measure of that value or the interpretation of the value in that moment. The price is what we pay and the value is what we get.[19]

---

[19] Think about the price of glass of water may have in the desert or at the North Pole

Circled Money

Thoughts on Economy and Business, Trading and Personal Finance

In any case, the less risky approach suggests a way of selecting shares with good fundamentals. There is no reason to think that a company with bad fundamentals will grow in the future, but the probability of a company with good fundamentals doing so is definitely higher. Therefore, the criteria to select the best shares for our investment will be based on buying those which hold:

- a higher Earnings Yield = EBIT / enterprise value (company market value + financial debts)

and

- a high Return On Capital = EBIT / (net fixed assets + working capital).[20]

3.2.2. Engaging the Markets

From my point of view, as well as of many others, prices trend of a shares constitutes the historical set of data that consolidate bases for new trends. If we look at the average of the FTSE MIB market's oscillations, we can say that the daily maximum oscillation is around 1%; which means that, in theory, we could potentially

---

[20] The Little Book That Still Beats the Market Hardcover – September 7, 2010 by Joel Greenblatt.

always buy at the minimum and sell at the maximum making 1% profit a day.

In reality, if we set our target to get 0.5% per day, this is already a potential gain of 110% per year. We do not need to make the 0.5% with one share only, but also with 5 shares of 0.1% for example. Of course, we need to consider trading commissions; but the model offer big potential if we thing that a good investment product gives 5% a year.

Once I have selected the shares with high Earnings Yield and high Return On Capital as described above, observed the range of operability (identifying supports and resistances), and studied the trends and the volumes, my method suggest to entry the market and buy with strong relative losses (1-2-3%) on generally losing days of the market and sell when my profit margins target are met. Until I achieve the minimum margins I am happy with (see chapter 3.3.1 below), if the negative trend continues, I buy, mediating with the following sequences:

- First Engagement: Buy the same volume at 2% loss so that the loss is reduced to close 1%.

- Second Engagement: Buy 2 times the initial volume at 3% loss so that the averaged loss is reduced to close 1.5%

Circled Money

Thoughts on Economy and Business, Trading and Personal Finance

- Third Engagement: Buy 4 times the initial volume at 4 % loss, so that the new averaged loss is reduced to close 2%

At the end of this sequence, we can still hope that a good session in the two following days put us in a situation to recover any losses and make some gains.

A method of identifying the best entry points comes from the Elliott Waves Theory.

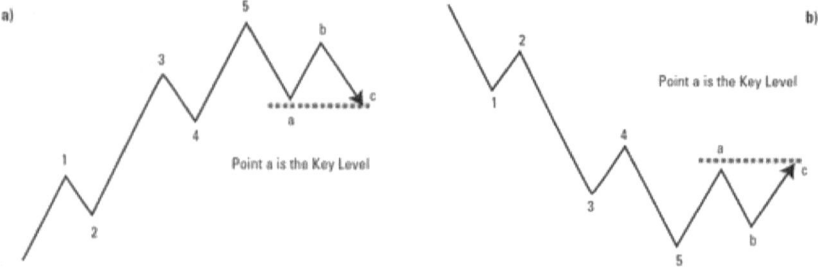

This theory says that there are usually five waves in a rise of 1-2-3-4-5, followed by three corrective waves or downwards a-b-c trends (see Figure a).

The cycle here is almost complete, and the behavior of the wave (c) is the key for reading the ongoing trend and predicting the next moves.

If it bounces at a level higher than (a), the uptrend is stable and we could consolidate profits and wait for the next downtrend.

If it falls below the minimum of the wave (a), this could be wave 3 in another movement of 5 waves (See Figure b), which gives a bearish signal; and therefore, it's an opportunity to accumulate.

The exposure of the first engagement depends very much on your risk acceptance and money availability.

It's not exactly the same, but this concept came to my mind by looking at the Martingale strategy which was once most commonly practiced in the gambling halls of Las Vegas casinos.

The problem with this strategy is that, to achieve 100% profitability, you need to have very deep pockets. The method in fact consist of doubling the bet after every loss.

In a binary system we have:

Stake	Outcome	Profit/Loss	Running Balance
$1	Win	$1	$1
$1	Win	$1	$2
$1	Lose	-$1	$1
$2	Lose	-$2	-$1
$4	Lose	-$4	-$5
$8	Win	$8	$3

In the gambling arena, this strategy is based on probability theory, and if your budget is good enough, this would enjoy a near 100% success rate[21].

---

[21] This is the main reason why casinos now have set minimums and maximums limits betting.

Circled Money

Thoughts on Economy and Business, Trading and Personal Finance

No one has infinite wealth, but with a theory that relies on mean reversion [22], one missed trade can bankrupt an entire account.

Another negative aspect is that the amount risked on the trade is far greater than the potential gain.

However, my method is not following 100% the Martingale and has the protection of shares fundamentally solid with long-term ascending trends and additional protections, set here in the following.

3.2.3. Protection

There are other two elements of protection suggested for the approach described before:

> 1. Being that the shares are chosen on the basis of their financial stability, there is, in the long run, a good probability that they will rise. This is like buying government or company bonds at lower price than their value of reimbursement at their expiration date. There will be a gain (unless the persistence of the inherent risks

---

[22] http://www.investopedia.com/terms/m/meanreversion.asp . Mean reversion is the theory suggesting that prices and returns eventually move back toward the mean or average. This mean or average can be the historical average of the price or return, or another relevant average such as economic growth or the average return of an industry

linked to every financial investment), it's just matter of time.

2. If even the expectations at point 1 will not materialize, we can consider the possibility of consolidating losses to compensate taxes on capital gains.

3. Straddle trade, with financial products with inverse relationships. If we open long & short positions at the same time on a products or buy financial products with negative correlation [23], we can manage the oscillations in such a way as to take profits from both the directions of the market.

If that doesn't bring the expected revenue, since the gains can be eaten by the losses, point 2 above can provide still a way out still with some positive outcomes (even if minimal).

---

[23] Swiss Franc vs. the Dollar Index, Gasoline vs. Natural Gas, Feeder Cattle vs. Feed Wheat, Cocoa vs. the NASDAQ 100 Index, Coffee vs. U.S. Treasury Notes, the British Pound vs. the Dollar Index, the Canadian Dollar vs. the Dollar Index, Gold vs. the Dollar Index, and the S&P 500 vs. Treasury Bonds.

3.3. EXECUTION

3.3.1. Margin setting

The real value of an asset is the value of work, which consists in a combination of material resources, know-how, and the time necessary to make it. The real price of everything (their sale or market prices) is dependent on Ask and Bid conditions, the effort and trouble of getting it (the real value, or how much effort it costs to procure it by itself), and other factors that are directly related to the characteristics of human beings (i.e. tendencies, trends and forecasts). The value of the goods that we acquire is the toil and trouble that we can save for ourselves (if we want to keep the goods for our own) and the relief from burdens which we can offer to others (if we decide to sell or trade it for another good).

Money saves the effort for procuring the good because they contain the value of a certain quantity of labor which we exchange for what we believe (in that moment) to contain an equal amount of value. Labor was the first price; the first currency of the original purchase that was paid for every good. The value of things that we own and want to trade is precisely equal to the amount of work that someone else puts in place to produce them or buy them or have them at their disposal. Although the work is the real measure of the exchange value of all commodities, it is not the measure according to which their value is commonly estimated. It is often difficult to establish the proportion between two different quantities of labor. The time spent in two different kinds of work will not always be sufficient to determine its value because it must also be taken into account the different degrees of difficulty and ingenuity to perform it. There may be more work in the hard work of an hour than in two hours of easy work; or in one hour of an application that costs ten years of studies than in a month of administrative work. It is not easy to find an accurate measure of both effort and ingenuity. However, by exchanging different products from different types of work, this is generally considered to be a combination of both of these factors. For a proper identification of the right margin to be established for the compensation of our trading activity we need to consider two additional variables: stress and pride. We will build a comparison matrix where we will break-down the 4 labor cost's components for few different professional activities and will use those parameters to set our target margin points. In order to do so, I will take, as a baseline, the figures (net values, without taxes)

Circled Money

Thoughts on Economy and Business, Trading and Personal Finance

representing the labor market that I know better, which is the work environment in Italy at the Economic Condition of 2016[24]. Let's assume that the medium standard salary of a permanently-employed individual with a master's degree qualification in the middle of his career path, is 39'000 Euro net per year. This means that he makes around 25 euro net per hour with a 70% time commitment (around 9 hours over a 14 productive hours a day). For our argument we will take as term of reference the following Work Revenue examples :

- The hourly rate of an independent generic hand worker that we call on occasion, like a mason or a painter (with practical experience but no high school education), is 30 Euro per hour.
- The hourly rate of an independent, specialized technician that we call on occasion, like an electrician or a plumber (with

---

[24] Let's make a quick hint to standard conditions in Switzerland we were referring to when I was part of a Lean Management Project:
- Shop Worker: 90 CHF/h
- Employee: 100 CHF/h
- Manager: 120 CHF/h
- Warehouse: 120 CHF/m2 per year
- Workshop:: 150 CHF/m2 per year
- Office: 200 CHF/m2 per year

experience and high school education, no university degree), is 40 Euro per hour.
- The hourly rate of an independent occasional worker, like an unprofessional cleaning lady (with no experience and no education), is 10 Euro per hour,

and the following of Capital Revenue case:
- The yield of a rented apartment (of the kind analyzed in Section Two) with initial investment of 150,000€, with a 90,000€ mortgage over 25 years, with a rental fee of 600€ per month, considering all accessory costs and taxes and a property annual re-evaluation of 1% per year, gives 900€ net per year. Its management requires around 3 hours a month, which results in 25 Euro per hour. At this point, we are able to give an hypothesis on what could be the right margin, considering that, as we said few lines above, the hourly rate is compounded by:
  - Effort,
  - Ingenuity,
  - Stress,

Circled Money

Thoughts on Economy and Business, Trading and Personal Finance

- less the relieving part (Pride, Satisfaction) [25] that offset the three previous burdens. In theory, I could do for free, something that I really like.

Being the final scope of this exercise of exclusive personal validity, the numbers given below are the result of a combination of my own vision of the labor market, my personality, and subjective considerations.

---

[25] This is the kind of value - wellness and interior fullness - that we feel when we do something that we like. It can be called a value of experience, which is difficult to measure and quantify in monetary terms, and has no objective criteria.

During my studies in Rome, I often bought my beer in a small grocery store in Via Labicana.

On one of the many Friday afternoons, the owner said to me: "Why don't you collect the caps? Then you can have the beers for free !? " And here I thought that I understood the border between unconditioned pleasures and drinking beer, which didn't include accumulating the caps to get more for free.

I was happy to pay for the beer just because that gesture was simply for the unique purpose of enjoying a beer. Since that time, I haven't bought beer anymore simply because:
1) I didn't want to drink beer just to collect caps, and
2) and once I had drunk a beer, I didn't want to regret if I didn't collect their caps.

The credit card company Mastercard made the "Priceless" principle one of its most successful marketing campaigns.

All this to say that conducting online trading or reading about economy are things that make me feel good and which contribute to lowering my trading margin expectations.

Net Values per Hour	Earning	Effort	Ingenuity	Stress	Pride
Employee	25	5	20	10	-10
Generic handworker	30	22	5	10	-7
Specialized technician	40	20	18	10	-8
House-cleaning Lady	10	9	1	4	-4
Rental Yield	25	5	18	10	-8

My perception of the cost of labor is the sum of the values on the lines per the columns Effort, Ingenuity, Stress & Pride.

Based on this assumption, I can consider my trading activity cost, as broken down below,

	Effort	Ingenuity	Stress	Pride
My Trading	5	20	10	-10

which sets my own margin at 25 Euro per trading hour (5+20+10-10).

3.3.2. Minimum Business Volumes & Operations

Since profitability also derives from the combination of the frequency and magnitude of gains and losses, then if, even with low margins, we can operate by increasing the number of operations (like a manual and slower HFT system), our likelihood of getting a multiplicity of reasonable margins rises even more.

Circled Money

Thoughts on Economy and Business, Trading and Personal Finance

The number of operations is linked to commission trading costs (say 0.195% - minimum 2.95 Euro per trade) and taxation (in Italy, 27% on shares sales profits).

0.195% equals the minimum of 2.95 Euro per trade, when the trade is around 1,500 Euro, which is the optimized value for my engagement. For an investment of 1,500 Euro in order to generate a 25Euro profit, it must rise by 1.66%, the range of bi-daily swings between the maximum and minimum of the FTSE-MIB in the latest years. Assuming that we will usually not buy at the minimum and sell at the maximum, the timeframe of our investment should be few days. If I am not able to make the 25 Euro gain, and shares go down, I buy the same amount of shares at 2% loss of their buying price; so I'll have an average loss close to 1%. If, again, I am not in the position of consolidating my own margin, I buy the same amount of shares in my wallet at 3% loss on the average price of my buying price; so I average the loss at 1.5%. If again, I am not in the position to consolidate my own margin, I buy the same amount of shares in my wallet at a 4% loss on my average price buying price, so to average a loss of 2%.

Until that point, we can still expect to recover a loss in the following two daily sessions, with the bounce described in Elliott's waves theory.

For a total investment of 6,000 Euro, though, I suggest to keep a liquidity margin of 24,000 Euro (1/5 ratio) to face any financial emergency in the following 12 months. Overall, if the shares selection has been done applying the criteria of Greenblatt's method, on the long term, you should be safe. To have a reasonable balance between risk and reward while increasing the exposure with progressive investments, I would raise my margin expectation as well. For an investment cumulated up to 6,000 Euro, I would wait to sell till I get a 50 Euro margin[26]; but that depends as well on individual sensitivity and the specific market conditions at that time. Of course, the amount of money we want to put on the plate depends very much on our capital asset availability and risk propensity, but the order of magnitude and proportions gives an idea on how we can set the strategy.

The target for my operations is their close after 1-3 accumulations (Buys) and 1 distribution (Sale). If these operations bring me a reward of 25 Euros target gain per hour of commitment (adding the small timeframes you take in the evening to set your sell and buy orders) this is for me a good reward.

---

[26] For a cumulative investment till 6'000 Euro I probably spent two hours of studies.

Circled Money

Thoughts on Economy and Business, Trading and Personal Finance

Many will shiver reading these words because professional traders often suggest not to cut gains and consider dangerous averaging on losses. I do it different and that's also freedom.

4. CONCLUSION

Assuming that in our own jobs we are paid for a service that we render to society, in the moment in which I consolidate a gain thanks to a simple speculative financial activity, how can I justify the ethical aspects of this operation?

Who gives us the right of making money without giving any added value or any contribution to the development of our community?

Shall we take it as if we won at the lottery?

In fact, we do not exchange money for goods; but money for money, and even when this is understood, it might be disliked by many.

It is a perception, but what people think about financial speculation and their sense of contempt, makes it even more attractive.

The opportunity of generating surplus thanks to my capital stock, without creating value, together with the uncertainty that my strategies will not necessarily lead to money gains, makes everything extremely challenging.

It's a bit like that instinctive feeling towards "easy money" without falling into illegality; but please let's not fall in error attempting to reduce it to the random element of a pure and simple bet.

Circled Money

Thoughts on Economy and Business, Trading and Personal Finance

We need to believe in the recurring cycles of natural events and become aware that in any case we walk on the edge of instability.

We must be ready to jump on the next train when the one we are riding is not fast enough. We need to be trained to manage changes and be ready to take on any new challenge, viewing it as a new opportunity.

Our goal is not to rely on fate, but on an array of probabilities that we can process creating a structured methodology that on average gives a more predictable result that just betting on odds and evens.

This is not the roulette. We do not win, but make gains; we do not lose, but we suffer losses.

We do not rely upon or believe in luck; it's all part of a huge system subject to thoughts and actions of humans in relation to emotions, fear, expectations and hopes.

To come back to our existential issue raised at the beginning of this chapter, let's console us with the fact that placement and displacement of our money adds liquidity to the market and have other direct and indirect effects.

For example: let's assume that I have a huge amount of money and I have no ideas, time, or opportunity to manage it.

At that same time, someone else might be in a totally different environment and mood and if I lend him my money, he could give it back to me plus a profit. He could have also created a gain for himself and for all those who interacted in his initiative.

The money created money and fueled the imagination to create value. In a regulated society where this value is in line with the law and the rules, this created a value for the community.

We are happier and we have easier access to primary assets like value in money and experience.

With the expansion of the general financial culture we will make prosperous investments, we will provide liquidity to the markets, foster scientific competition, and raise the level of the technology. We will invent new products, will satisfy new needs and generate revenues for all and for us to reinvest. This will keep the system moving until we will find the new edges of the science and will master absolute knowledge.

I hope to have stimulated the financial sensitivity of my readers with the purpose that this book can suggest a wiser management of capital asset resources and develop a common, rational and sustainable wealthiness.

Circled Money

Thoughts on Economy and Business, Trading and Personal Finance

ACKNOWLEDGMENTS

I owe everything to my wife Valentina, with which I conceived the foundations for the affections and financial stability of our family. She is a precious source of peace and inspiration for the materialization of my ideas and projects.

BIBLIOGRAPHY & DEEPENINGS

Books

Benetazzo, E. (2010). *PADRONE DEL TUO DENARO*. Milano, Italia: Sperling & Kupler.

Wolman, W., & Colamosca, A. (1997). *IL TRADIMENTO DELL'ECONOMIA*. Milano, Italia: Ponte Alle Grazie.

Gorini, R. (2014). *MATRIX ECONOMY*. Cesena, Italia: ESSERE FELICI.

Greenblatt, J. (2007). *IL PICCOLO LIBRO CHE BATTE IL MERCATO AZIONARIO*. Milano, Italia: CHW Edizioni di Cinehollywood Srl.

Piketty, T. (2014). *IL CAPITALE nel XXI secolo*. Milano, Italia: Bompiani/RCS Libri S.p.A..

Rampini, F. (2014). *All You Need Is Love*. Milano, Italia: Arnoldo Mondadori Editore S.p.A..

Smith, A. (2006). *La ricchezza delle nazioni* (4th ed.). Novara, Italia: Istituto Geografico De Agostini S.p.A..

Varoufakis, Y. (2015). *E' L'ECONOMIA CHE CAMBIA IL MONDO*. Milano, Italia: RCS Libri S.p.A.

Magazines and Internet Sources

[Analisi dei volumi]. (2012). Retrieved from https://www.meteofinanza.com/guadagnare-lanalisi-volume-dei-prezzi/

Angiolini, A. (2015, December). Trading Robot. *Traders*, 4(1), 20-22.

Calabria, M. A. (2015, October). Society, Finance & Freedom. *BANKING PERSPECTIVE*, 3(4), 51-58.

Cecchetti, S. G. (2015, October). Shadow Banking. *BANKING PERSPECTIVE*, 3(4), 42-48.

Circled Money

Thoughts on Economy and Business, Trading and Personal Finance

[Cooperativa Agricola Canedo]. (2012). Retrieved from http://www.canedo.it/how-cmsms-works.html

Galimberti, F. (2016, July). La concorrenza perfetta. *Il Sole 24 Ore, 11*(1), 6-17.

Galimberti, F. (2016, July). Il dilemma del Pil. *Il Sole 24 Ore, 11*(1), 18-23.

Hanna, R. (2015, December). Fare trading con un vantaggio statistico. *Traders, 4*(1), 36-38.

Levince, R. (2015, October). Banking on Prosperity. *BANKING PERSPECTIVE, 3*(4), 21-30.

Longo F. (2015, March). Volumi, Accumulazione e Distribuzione. Retrieved from https://www.fabiolongo.com/borsa/volumi.html

Maisano, L. (2016, October 08). Sterlina in caduta libera per un «flash crash». Retrieved from http://www.ilsole24ore.com/art/mondo/2016-10-08/sterlina-caduta-libera-un-flash-crash-081026.shtml?uuid=ADhtKZYB

Moltrasio, B. (2015, December 10). Il Volume di Scambio: il migliore amico del Trader. Retrieved from https://universitrading.com/il-volume-di-scambio-il-migliore-amico-del-trader/

Nojin, P. (2015, December). Il trading tecnico funziona. *Traders, 4*(1), 44-46.

Okopedia. (2014, November 15). Produttività marginale. Retrieved from http://www.okpedia.it/produttivita_marginale

Okopedia. (2014, November 15). Funzione di produzione. Retrieved from http://www.okpedia.it/funzione_di_produzione

Wright, R. E. (2015, October). Finance and Society : a Historical Perspective. *BANKING PERSPECTIVE, 3*(4), 33-40.